`burn

Much Ado About Nothing

ARDEN STUDENT SKILLS
LANGUAGE AND WRITING

Series Editor

Dympna Callaghan, Syracuse University

Published Titles

Antony and Cleopatra, Virginia Mason Vaughan
Hamlet, Dympna Callaghan
Macbeth, Emma Smith
Othello, Laurie Maguire
Romeo and Juliet, Catherine Belsey
The Tempest, Brinda Charry
Twelfth Night, Frances E. Dolan

Forthcoming Titles

King Lear, Jean Howard
A Midsummer Night's Dream, Heidi Brayman Hackel
The Merchant of Venice, Douglas Lanier

Much Ado About Nothing

Language and Writing

INDIRA GHOSE

Bloomsbury Arden Shakespeare
An imprint of Bloomsbury Publishing Plc

B L O O M S B U R Y

LONDON · OXFORD · NEW YORK · NEW DELHI · SYDNEY

Bloomsbury Arden Shakespeare

An imprint of Bloomsbury Publishing Plc

Imprint previously known as Arden Shakespeare

50 Bedford Square	1385 Broadway
London	New York
WC1B 3DP	NY 10018
UK	USA

www.bloomsbury.com

BLOOMSBURY, THE ARDEN SHAKESPEARE and the Diana logo are trademarks of Bloomsbury Publishing Plc

First published 2018

British Library Cataloguing-in-Publication Data
A catalogue record for this book is available from the British Library.

ISBN:	HB:	978-1-472-58098-6
	PB:	978-1-472-58097-9
	ePDF:	978-1-472-58100-6
	eBook:	978-1-472-58099-3

Library of Congress Cataloging-in-Publication Data
Names: Ghose, Indira, author.
Title: Much ado about nothing : language and writing / Indira Ghose.
Description: London ; New York : Bloomsbury Arden Shakespeare, 2017. |
Series: Arden student skills: language and writing | Includes bibliographical references.
Identifiers: LCCN 2017012856| ISBN 9781472580979 (paperback) | ISBN 9781472580986 (hardback)
Subjects: LCSH: Shakespeare, William, 1564-1616. Much ado about nothing. | Shakespeare, William, 1564-1616--Language. | BISAC: DRAMA / Shakespeare. | LITERARY CRITICISM / Shakespeare.
Classification: LCC PR2828 .G45 2017 | DDC 822.3/3--dc23 LC record available at https://lccn.loc.gov/2017012856

Series: Arden Student Skills: Language and Writing

Cover design: Irene Martinez Costa
Cover image © The Folger Shakespeare Library

Typeset by Fakenham Prepress Solutions, Fakenham, Norfolk NR21 8NN
Printed and bound in Great Britain

To find out more about our authors and books visit www.bloomsbury.com. Here you will find extracts, author interviews, details of forthcoming events and the option to sign up for our newsletters.

CONTENTS

SERIES EDITOR'S PREFACE

This series puts the pedagogical expertise of distinguished literary critics at the disposal of students embarking upon Shakespeare Studies at university. While they demonstrate a variety of approaches to the plays, all the contributors to the series share a deep commitment to teaching and a wealth of knowledge about the culture and history of Shakespeare's England. The approach of each of the volumes is direct yet intellectually sophisticated and tackles the challenges Shakespeare presents. These volumes do not provide a shortcut to Shakespeare's works, but instead offer a careful explication of them directed towards students' own processing and interpretation of the plays and poems.

Students' needs in relation to Shakespeare revolve overwhelmingly around language, and Shakespeare's language is what most distinguishes him from his rivals and collaborators. It also most embeds him in his own historical moment. The *Language and Writing* series understands language as the very heart of Shakespeare's literary achievement rather than as an obstacle to be circumvented. This series addresses the difficulties often encountered in reading Shakespeare alongside the necessity of writing papers for university examinations and course assessment. The primary objective here is to foster rigorous critical engagement with the texts by helping students develop their own critical writing skills. *Language and Writing* titles demonstrate how to develop students' own capacity to articulate and enlarge upon their experience of encountering the text, far beyond summarizing, paraphrasing or 'translating' Shakespeare's language into a more palatable

contemporary form. Each of the volumes in the series introduces the text as an act of specifically literary language and
shows that the multifarious issues of life and history that
Shakespeare's work addresses cannot be separated from their
expression in language. In addition, each book takes students
through a series of guidelines about how to develop viable
undergraduate critical essays on the text in question, not by
delivering interpretations, but rather by taking readers step by
step through the process of discovering and developing their
own critical ideas.

All the books include chapters examining the text from the
point of view of its composition, that is, from the perspective
of Shakespeare's own process of composition as a reader,
thinker and writer. The opening chapters consider when and
how the play was written, addressing, for example, the extant
literary and cultural acts of language from which Shakespeare
constructed his work – including his sources – as well as the
generic literary and theatrical conventions at his disposal.
Subsequent sections demonstrate how to engage in detailed
examination and analysis of the text and focus on the literary,
technical and historical intricacies of Shakespeare's verse and
prose. Each volume also includes some discussion of performance. Other chapters cover textual issues as well as the
interpretation of the extant texts for any given play on stage
and screen, treating, for example, the use of stage directions
or parts of the play that are typically cut in performance.
Authors also address issues of stage/film history as they relate
to the cultural evolution of Shakespeare's words. In addition,
these chapters deal with the critical reception of the work,
particularly the newer theoretical and historicist approaches
that have revolutionized our understanding of Shakespeare's
language over the past forty years. Crucially, every chapter
contains a section on 'Writing matters', which links the
analysis of Shakespeare's language with students' own critical
writing.

The series empowers students to read and write about
Shakespeare with scholarly confidence and hopes to inspire

their enthusiasm for doing so. The authors in this series have been selected because they combine scholarly distinction with outstanding teaching skills. Each book exposes the reader to an eminent scholar's teaching in action and expresses a vocational commitment to making Shakespeare accessible to a new generation of student readers.

Professor Dympna Callaghan
Series Editor
Arden Student Skills: Language and Writing

PREFACE

Much Ado About Nothing is a romantic comedy that scintil-
lates with wit and laughter and captivates audiences with
its engaging characters. Its dazzling surface might seduce us
into thinking it is all style and little substance; however, its
title notwithstanding, it is not a play about trivialities. On
the contrary, it is about large issues: honour and dishonour,
relationships between men and women, and the correspondence
between seeming and being, appearances and reality. The title
of the play encapsulates the main themes in a multi-layered
pun. In addition to a trifle, the term 'nothing' could refer to
women's sexuality and to noting or watching. Thus, the title
of the play gestures towards the elaborate cult of honour that
exerted such a powerful grip on early modern society. For
a woman, honour referred above all to her chastity. Even
the breath of suspicion that she might have been disloyal
would single her out for public shaming. The Renaissance
concept of honour was inextricably interwoven with the
culture of courtesy that had taken hold of Europe, inspired
by Castiglione's influential work *The Book of the Courtier*
(1528). The play presents a setting in which gracious manners,
an attractive exterior and elegant language were the marks of
a cultivated society, a society in which producing a glittering
façade was of central importance and whose hallmarks were
observing others and, conversely, being the constant centre of
social attention. *Much Ado About Nothing* is also a play that
has given us Beatrice and Benedick, one of the most delightful
pair of lovers in Shakespeare's comedies. The pun in the play's
title seems to endorse their view of romance, nonchalantly
shrugging off the obsession of their peers with the cult of
honour as well as the romantic clichés that pervaded society.

This book cannot examine these issues in any great depth, but it does hope to encourage the reader to reflect on the myriad facets of this text by tapping into several important aspects and providing a historical context for its main concerns. In the Introduction, we discuss the question of genre, and whether the play contains tragic as well as comic elements. We also scrutinize the way Shakespeare has diverged from his source material. In Chapter 1, we examine the setting of the play and the way the Renaissance culture of courtesy forms the backdrop of its events. The remainder of the chapter looks closely at the language of the play, focusing on wit, repartee and malapropism as the main linguistic devices. The chapter ends with a consideration of the comic subplot of the play and how Shakespeare's humour might have emerged out of the theatrical conditions of his time, with clown roles written to order for specific star comedians.

In Chapter 2, we begin with a brief overview of the importance of rhetoric in early modern culture. Rhetorical strategies in *Much Ado About Nothing* include the idea of exploring questions from various angles, a key notion in theories of rhetoric. *Much Ado About Nothing* is written predominantly in prose. An analysis of some of the features of theatrical prose in this period is followed by a reflection on what effect shifting between the modes of prose and verse might have. Next, we look at examples of imagery in the play, and in particular at the controlling metaphor of fashion. Finally, we consider the way Shakespeare uses language in characterization, focusing on one example.

Chapter 3 takes a closer look at the central themes the play explores. These are hinted at in the pun that the title contains. This section reviews the Renaissance concept of honour and what it implies for men and for women. It also probes the question of appearances and briefly elaborates on the debate about fraudulent façades that was raging in this period, which saw a concerted attack on idolatry throughout Protestant Europe. In point of fact, the controversy about surface impressions as opposed to intrinsic truths harks back to the argument put forward by Plato in his dialogue *Gorgias*. Plato had thrown up the question as to whether artful language was purely ornamental and simply a means to produce gratification, or whether it was an agent of truth and virtue. Shakespeare's culture, marked as it was by a resurgence of rhetoric, was preoccupied with the same question. The play approaches the issue of surfaces and reality from a range of angles. By calling attention to its own status as a pleasing fiction, it extends the interrogation of the play to the role of theatrical illusion itself.

Chapter 4 expands the purview of the discussion to include analysis of performances of the play. It suggests several topics into which it might be interesting to delve in connection with recent film versions and stage productions of *Much Ado About Nothing*. Building on the extensive advice provided in the other volumes in this series on how to write a research essay, this book reiterates a few key suggestions.

Introduction

Much Ado About Nothing: Comic or tragic?

Much Ado About Nothing is a romantic comedy filled with love and laughter, a play that sparkles with wit and glitters with a coterie of beautiful people distinguished by their exquisite manners. At the same time, it hints at a darkness lingering just beyond the frame of the comic action, and its elegant language is laced with violence and cruelty. The blending of light and shade, gaiety and pain, is a typical feature of Shakespeare's comedies, but comes to the fore particularly in the plays that have been termed the 'mature' comedies: *Much Ado About Nothing*, *As You Like It* and *Twelfth Night*.

Not all ages have admired this feature of Shakespeare's work. The critic Thomas Rymer, who introduced French neoclassical norms into England, was scathing about the mixture of comic and tragic elements in his plays. Adherents of neoclassicist ideas insisted that comedies were comedies and tragedies were tragedies, and never the twain should meet. They declared that Shakespeare's penchant for inserting moments of darkness into his comedies – and scenes of grotesque humour into his tragedies – was an unforgivable breach of decorum. Decorum, an idea that had been discussed at length by ancient philosophers and thinkers, meant something different from its present-day meaning of dignified behaviour. It was an aesthetic principle that demanded that every artist adopt a style appropriate to the subject matter being treated, be it in a play, in visual art or in poetic language.

It was also a rule that applied in rhetoric. As rhetoricians made clear, orators were expected to select a type of speech suited to the topic in hand from a variety of styles ranging from 'low' to 'middle' to 'high'. When talking about a serious theme, the appropriate style was elevated and dignified; when speaking of trivial affairs, a lighter mode was suitable. For the ancients, adjusting one's style to the matter in hand was not merely an aesthetic doctrine: it was an ethical precept. Propriety implied harmony, and harmony and order were two of the most exalted ideals in Greek and Roman thought. They formed the basis of the order of the universe itself. Balance and symmetry in one's behaviour, and by analogy in works of art, chimed with the vision of natural order that most ancient philosophers shared. Plato was the first to formulate the four cardinal virtues – prudence, justice, fortitude and temperance. In his ethical guidebook *De Officiis* [*On Obligations*], which remained highly popular throughout the Middle Ages and the Renaissance, Cicero even replaced temperance (or moderation) with the Latin term 'decorum'. Cicero's own source was the Greek Stoic philosopher Panaetius, and, like Panaetius, Cicero insisted that decorum govern all the virtues.

In literature, decorum meant that there should be a correspondence between genres and their subject matter, characters and style. Tragedies should represent noble characters and elevated themes; comedies should restrict themselves to more frivolous topics and less exalted persons. The early modern period was one characterized by an avid desire to emulate the ideas of classical antiquity – the term 'Renaissance' referred above all to the 'rebirth' of classical thought. Writers such as Ben Jonson did in fact attempt to adhere to neoclassical norms and keep tragic and comic material strictly separate from each other. Shakespeare, however, broke every rule in the neoclassical book. Hamlet (clearly an admirer of neoclassical rules) admonishes the travelling players who come to Elsinore and are preparing to stage a theatrical performance to 'Suit the action to the word, the word to the action' (3.2.17–18), but the play bearing his name is anything but a model of decorous theatricality. Hamlet himself careens between being wildly funny and desperately desolate; the play was excoriated by Voltaire precisely because it transgressed classical decorum by including a grotesque scene in which a prince juggles with skulls in a graveyard, enters into a battle of wits with a lowly gravedigger, and ends up being bested by him into the bargain. Shakespeare's tragedies consistently infringe the rules of decorum by incorporating bouts of dark humour into their plots or placing a fool centre stage at crucial moments. In *Macbeth*, a porter cracks dirty jokes immediately after a king has been murdered; in *King Lear*, a court jester accompanies Lear in the climactic storm scene, and keeps up a running commentary of riddles and taunts aimed at the king throughout the first half of the play. In *Antony and Cleopatra*, just before Cleopatra stages the operatic spectacle of her own death, a clown comes on stage and makes a few wisecracks about the poisonous snakes hidden in the basket he has brought her. In *Othello*, the malevolent mischief-maker Iago is also a consummate comic entertainer, who seduces the audience into a sense of complicity with his diabolical plans. His ingenuity in manipulating people, his brilliance in plotting, and his obvious delight in his skills are infectious. On another level, the tragic hero himself loses every shred of dignity when he falls victim to an epileptic fit brought on by his sheer gullibility for Iago's poisonous insinuations against his wife. He turns into a ridiculous figure, reminiscent of the stock jestbook persona of an aging husband cuckolded by his young wife. But just as the tragedies often veer close to the ludicrous, so dark shadows frequently hover over the comedies. In fact, the comic world often teeters on the brink of tragedy. In *A Midsummer Night's Dream*, the lovers stumble into a nightmare scenario of hate and betrayal in the Athenian woods, and a tragic outcome is averted only thanks to the intervention of the king of the fairies, Oberon. *The Two Gentlemen of Verona* ends with a narrow escape from rape, *Love's Labour's Lost* with a death. *The Comedy of Errors* is built around the plot device of mistaken identity, which is portrayed so hauntingly that even the happy end does not quite dissolve the impression of the pain and bewilderment felt by characters who suddenly lose any sense of who they are.

At a closer look, the stories Shakespeare's comedies tell are often uncannily close to those of his tragedies. In *Much Ado About Nothing*, the plot turns on sexual jealousy and the misinterpretation of signs by the suspicious lover and his supporters, who erroneously leap to the conclusion that he has been betrayed. A few years later, Shakespeare would reuse the material, first in a tragedy, *Othello*, and then in a romance (or tragi-comedy), *The Winter's Tale*. The tragic ending that is narrowly avoided in *Much Ado About Nothing* is played out to the full in *Othello*, which ends with a stage littered with corpses. In *The Winter's Tale*, Leontes orders the death of his wife, Hermione, in a stage-managed trial, but is thwarted at the last moment by the noblewoman Paulina, who manages to spirit Hermione away and hide her for sixteen years. The married couple are reunited at the end, but the price they pay in terms of torment and suffering is a high one. In Plato's *Symposium*, the very distinction between comic and tragic material is called into question. At the end of a long, wine-soaked night of endless conversation, Socrates turns to Agathon and Aristophanes, two dramatists of ancient Greece (the first specializing in tragedy, the second in comedy), and draws them to admit that the difference in the way they practise their craft is superficial. And on a slightly less elevated note, the comedian Mel Brooks tackles the same question. He explains the vital difference between comedy and tragedy as follows: 'Tragedy is when I cut my finger. Comedy is when you fall into an open sewer and die.' As so often, jokes contain a nugget of wisdom buried in layers of absurdity. Whether something is comic or tragic really boils down to a matter of perspective.

Perhaps the most resounding blow in defence of Shakespeare's rejection of strict boundaries between the comic and the tragic was dealt by the great eighteenth-century critic Dr Samuel Johnson. In his Preface *The Plays of William Shakespeare*, he writes,

Shakespeare's plays are not in the rigorous and critical sense either tragedies or comedies, but compositions of a distinct kind; exhibiting the real state of sublunary nature, which partakes of good and evil, joy and sorrow, mingled with endless variety of proportion and innumerable modes of combination; and expressing the course of the world, in which the loss of one is the gain of another; in which, at the same time, the reveller is hasting to his wine and the mourner burying his friend; in which the malignity of one is sometimes defeated by the frolick of another; and many mischiefs and many benefits are done and hindered without design. (1977: 303–4)

For Dr Johnson, Shakespeare plays, both tragic and comic, mirror the immutable human condition. The world is a place where happiness and pain exist side by side, and where some people suffer while others are celebrating life; for every human being who dies, someone somewhere is being born. Moreover, as he points out, we are not in complete control of our lives. Chance and fortune play a significant role in shaping the outcome of events, however much we might plot and plan in advance. In this way, both Shakespeare's tragedies and his comedies are true to life, however contrived the stories they are built around might be. If they consist of a blend of comic and tragic elements, this is an exact reflection of real life. Dr Johnson's justification of Shakespeare's generic mixture was decisive in deflecting criticism of the plays on the grounds of not fitting easily into the classical literary moulds of either tragedy or comedy, but combining features from both genres. Barbara Everett, in her essay '*Much Ado About Nothing*: The Unsociable Comedy' (2001), points out that the fusion of light and dark, seriousness and laughter is one of the essential principles that underlie Shakespearean comedy. To be more precise: the joyous moments evoked by the comedies only gain their power against the backdrop of potential tragedy and the bitterness of human life. As she puts it, 'The mature comedies seek to perfect a style or condition in which happiness exists

not just despite unhappiness but through it, because of it …
There must in the end be the co-existence, the smiling and the
grief' (Everett 2001: 60). And the Freudian critic Ernst Kris
reminds us that human beings are eternal pleasure seekers
'walking on a narrow ledge above an abyss of fear' (qtd in
Nelson 1990: 8). The darkness infusing *Much Ado About
Nothing* might be what makes it so magical.

Much Ado About Nothing and Shakespearean comedy

In many ways, *Much Ado About Nothing* is unique among
the group of romantic comedies with which it is usually
bracketed. Influential critics, in particular C. L. Barber, have
compared Shakespeare's comedies to early modern festivity.
Popular festivity was an important part of pre-Reformation
life throughout Europe, and many holy days dotted the
calendar year (see Burke 1978; Hutton 1994). These days
were not only celebrated with church services, but also served
as a pretext for general merry-making. One of the goals
of the Reformers was to rein in the widespread disorder-
liness associated with festive events. An enduring theme was
'misrule', which meant turning rules and regulations on their
head and the world upside down. The Church was by no
means immune to the spirit of disorder – on festive occasions,
junior clergy mocked their superiors by dressing up, braying
like donkeys, and parodying the traditional liturgy in other
inventive and what might seem to us strange and sacrilegious
ways. Reformers like Erasmus anticipated the modern outlook
by suspecting that many of the festive rituals were of pagan
origin. But this view was not one that most people in the
medieval world would understand. Anthropologists detect
similarities between Christian festivity in the Middle Ages
and carnival celebrations in other cultures. What they have in
common is the function of a safety valve – they allowed people

in an authoritarian society to let off steam. Far from threatening the strict hierarchies existing in these societies, regular opportunities for unruly conduct actually served to shore up the stern discipline that prevailed once things returned to normal in everyday life. But festivals could also offer an opportunity for protest and political critique, often expressed in satirical processions. Conversely, political revolts often borrowed the symbolism of carnival, and rioters articulated their challenge to authority in the form of festive masquerade.

In many parts of Europe, carnival was a season of riotous celebrations that occurred just before Lent, a period of penance and devotion that lasted six weeks and was intended to commemorate the forty days of fasting Christ underwent in the desert after his baptism and before the start of his ministry. Carnival was a time of excessive celebration: gluttony and other joys of the flesh were enthusiastically indulged in, and games and mumming (folk plays) were staged in abundance. In England, carnival celebrations were not associated with a certain time of year – they were a characteristic of all types of festivity. On all important holidays, processions, Morris dances and plays of various kinds took place. Probably the most important were the biblical plays put on at Corpus Christi, famously in York and Coventry, which dramatized the Passion of Christ.

The Reformation saw a sharp decline in popular festivities of all kinds. Ecclesiastic and secular authorities had long regarded the feasting, dances and games related to holy days with fear and suspicion. As they noted, holiday celebrations encouraged crime and anarchic behaviour, and to their mind bore the seeds of political subversion. Humanist thinkers were keen not only to revitalize Christianity and cleanse it of corrupted customs, but also to reform the mores of humanity in general. Puritans stressed the importance of discipline and working hard at one's vocation and advocated a drastic reduction in the number of holy days. This meshed with the changes in economic patterns that were introduced with the emergent market economy, which required a far more regular rhythm of work and leisure than in earlier forms of productivity (Thomas 1964). The most interesting change for our purposes was the banning of religious theatre and ritual plays. The form of Calvinism that took hold in England condemned liturgical drama as a kind of idolatry. Moreover, combining the sacred with the profane was now deemed unacceptable. But popular drama, far from dying out, found a new lease of life in the commercial theatre of the metropolis.

This is, of course, a simplified version of the development of the professional stage in the early modern period. There were intermediate phases, when interludes were staged in the halls of great houses and were attended by both aristocratic society and a large number of their retainers. These plays, like the morality plays that replaced the religious drama during the fifteenth century, formed a transition between biblical plays and the plays of the public stage in the early modern age. They were staged by quasi-professional actors and often presented allegories that set out to impart moral lessons. Furthermore, by no means all Protestant thinkers were hostile to the theatre. John Calvin encouraged plays for didactic purposes and the Genevan theologian Theodore Beza even supported transvestism on stage, which was anathema to Puritan divines in England, where all female roles were played by boy actors. Critics have argued that the virulent attacks on the theatre that circulated in England might have been bound up with the nature of the commercial stage in London (see Hawkes 2001). What is important to remember is the fact that even if the English Renaissance is not associated with a flourishing of the visual arts as in Italy, it was the birthplace of the professional popular theatre. The theatres in London, the first of which was founded in the 1570s, formed the kernel of the first vastly profitable entertainment industry that the world was to witness. Shakespeare and his company, the Lord Chamberlain's Men, were at the heart of this new mode of popular amusement.

If festive celebrations were on the wane in rural society, critics have argued, many of the features of festivity were imported into the professional theatre (Barber 1972). The comedies in particular embody a holiday atmosphere in which norms are upended in a topsy-turvy playworld, only to be restored in a denouement that exemplified harmony and social reconciliation. In the marriages with which the plays frequently ended, the social order was reaffirmed. During the course of the play, however, everything was up for grabs. Children defied their parents, girls dressed up as boys, queens fell in love with working-class men, women outwitted men and friends betrayed each other. The scholar Herman Northrop Frye has dubbed this world of comic inversion of rules and challenges to authority a 'green world' and detects a pattern at work in which the protagonists enter a magical universe of freedom from social restraint and plunge into dizzying adventures that call all certainties into question. Importantly, the exhilarating experience of the 'green world' is only a temporal one – the characters return to an orderly life at the end of the play. This framework is a perfect fit for *A Midsummer Night's Dream*, and critics have pinned down a 'green world' in the Forest of Arden (*As You Like It*), in Belmont (*The Merchant of Venice*) and even in the imaginary realm of Illyria (*Twelfth Night*). But as so often with Shakespeare, his work never quite fits the mould. In point of fact, it is illusory to generalize about Shakespearean comedy, as I have been doing. Each comedy is different. And *Much Ado About Nothing* certainly provides nothing remotely like a 'green world' of liberation for its characters.

Another typical feature of popular festivity was amateur theatricals – mummers putting on plays, revellers donning disguises, men dressing up as women. Particularly May games were associated with Robin Hood plays, in which a ribald 'Maid Marian' was a chief attraction. Shakespeare might have been inspired by the tradition of cross-dressing in his fondness for the idea of heroines slipping into male clothing, as he recycles the plot device in five plays – four comedies, *The Two Gentlemen of Verona*, *The Merchant of Venice*, *As You Like It* and *Twelfth Night*, and one romance, *Cymbeline*. This is partly because it is ideally suited to the spirited, courageous and quick-witted heroines in which the comedies abound. *Much Ado About Nothing* features one of his most brilliant and lively female creations, Beatrice, but she has no need to assume a disguise to prove her feistiness to the audience.

This is not to say that Shakespeare did not borrow traits from popular culture in this play. He had a magpie-like penchant for picking and choosing elements from the entire range of cultural paradigms on offer, and a gift for incorporating them into a unique blend of his own creation. *Much Ado About Nothing* does feature numerous themes and devices from folk culture, above all the incessant jokes about cuckoldry that were such a mainstay of jestbooks of the time. As it happens, this is the only Shakespearean play to mention a jestbook by name, *The Hundred Merry Tales*, although not in a complimentary manner. Beatrice is mortally insulted when she learns that Benedick has been denigrating her wit by spreading the word that she has borrowed all her ideas from the famous jestbook (2.1.117–18), which, by the time Shakespeare wrote his play, had become a byword for musty, outdated humour – nothing ages faster. The idea of a fake funeral and the resurrection of a character thought to be dead is another typical motif taken from popular comedy. We need to bear in mind, however, that the rigid divide between popular and high culture was only gradually coming into place (Burke 1978). In this period, the boundaries were still far more porous than in later periods. Jestbooks were items that the elite cherished, and some of the cleverest minds of the time, like Sir Thomas More and his friend Erasmus, delighted in collecting jokes and quips and riddles. The battle of the sexes, reflected in the sparring between Beatrice and Benedick, was a perennial topic in both popular and high culture, and found its way into cheap print as well as learned debates. The chief clown in *Much Ado About Nothing*, Dogberry, accurately mirrors the amalgam of different cultures that Shakespeare's drama personifies, for what is mainly funny about him is less his stupidity and overbearing pomposity than his desperate attempt to ape his betters. The method Shakespeare uses to mock him is satirizing his language.

What is striking about *Much Ado About Nothing* is its preoccupation with language. A high percentage of the lines (around 70 per cent) are in prose. In this respect, it resembles the plays Shakespeare probably wrote immediately beforehand – *Henry IV Parts 1* and *2* and *The Merry Wives of Windsor* – all of which demonstrate his interest in using prose in ingenious ways. The other 'mature' comedies that are usually grouped together with *Much Ado About Nothing*, *As You Like It* and *Twelfth Night*, which were written in the same period of Shakespeare's career, also contain many scenes in prose. Prose does not mean that the style is colloquial or that the characters speak in everyday language. The prose in the play is a polished, highly wrought product, based on models such as Ciceronian rhetoric and a refined style of writing known as euphuism, particularly popular in court circles in the 1580s. The language in the play ranges from dazzling repartee, puns and innuendo to elaborate metaphor and a barrage of rhetorical devices, and all this in prose. In addition, there are passages of emotional intensity in blank verse, a truncated sonnet and two songs – a wistful air and a dirge – all in rhyme. To round things off, the play contains a flood of examples of mangled words known as malapropisms. These diverse linguistic forms will be discussed in more details in the following chapters. At this stage, it might be worth bearing in mind that this is a play that explores language from various angles. Besides demonstrating a gamut of linguistic styles, the play takes as one of its main themes the use and abuse of language – how words can be deployed to achieve wide-reaching effects, both benign and malign, and the complex relationship they have with reality. The text that it resembles most in this respect, *Love's Labour's Lost*, was written a few years before *Much Ado About Nothing* and is another play whose specific focus, from a variety of perspectives, is language, even though verse predominates in the earlier play. Some critics believe that

Much Ado About Nothing is the lost comedy by Shakespeare
that is mentioned in the series of plays listed by Francis Meres
in his commonplace book *Palladis Tamia: Wits Treasury*
(1598), an important source in establishing the chronology of
Shakespeare's works. Meres included the title of an unknown
drama, *Love's Labour's Won*. The similarity between *Much
Ado About Nothing* and the earlier *Love's Labour's Lost* –
which also stars a pair of witty lovers, Rosaline and Berowne,
who engage in a skirmish of words, as well as eavesdropping
scenes and a masque – is so tantalizing that in 2014 the
Royal Shakespeare Company staged both plays in tandem,
both directed by Christopher Luscombe and with the exact
same cast of actors, re-baptizing *Much Ado About Nothing*
as *Love's Labour's Won*.

Sources of the play

Love's Labour's Lost is usually named as one of the few
plays by Shakespeare without any definitive source. The
main plot of *Much Ado About Nothing*, on the other hand,
is derived from a story that was frequently recycled both
in the form of poems and plays. The best-known version is
in Canto V of the epic poem by the celebrated Italian poet
Ludovico Ariosto, *Orlando Furioso*, which appeared in 1516
and was widely circulated even before being translated into
English by Sir John Harington in 1591. Spenser adapted the
tale into a tragic story in his own epic poem, *The Faerie
Queene* (1590). The same narrative appeared in a collection
of *novelle* (or tales) published by Matteo Bandello in 1554.
These stories were indispensable as source material for
English Renaissance drama and were plundered not only by
Shakespeare, but also by dramatists such as John Webster,
Philip Massinger and John Fletcher. The early modern
theatre was a vast entertainment machinery with a voracious
appetite for new material, especially since the staples of

medieval drama, biblical stories and saints' lore, were no longer permissible. Bandello's stories circulated in a French version (by François de Belleforest) before being 'Englished' by William Paynter in his collection *The Palace of Pleasure*, which appeared in two volumes in 1566 and 1567. The importance of Italianate literature in Elizabethan England can hardly be overemphasized. Between the 1560s and the 1660s over 400 titles were translated from the Italian, by over 200 authors (Fox 1997: 15). To a remarkable degree, English literature was formed through a process of assimilation and creative adaptation of Italian sources. A case in point is Shakespeare's reworking of his source material in *Much Ado About Nothing*.

Shakespeare made numerous changes to the story he had inherited, some mere adjustments in tone, but others of wider significance. Perhaps one of the most important is the way he alters the figure of the chief villain Don John. In the source stories, the person who maligns the heroine is a disappointed rival in love who takes revenge for being rejected by trying to humiliate the lovers and irrevocably harm the reputation of the female protagonist. By removing this motivation from Don John, Shakespeare remains true to his preference for avoiding simple explanations for human behaviour. As early as the age of Romanticism, critics had noted that in *Othello* Iago's destructive rage is out of all proportion to his alleged slights by the general. In his copy of the play, Samuel Taylor Coleridge scribbled the phrase 'motiveless malignity' to describe the depths of unexplained malevolence that seems to inspire Iago. It became a catchword for generations of critics. Don John is only a pale version of Iago, but he gains in psychological depth by the removal of a single driving motivation for his deeds. Admittedly, Don John is not a character of great complexity. Nevertheless, the play does provide hints at what might be at work in his mind at a deeper level and how this might echo larger concerns of the play. In Act 1 we overhear a fragment of conversation between Don John and his companion, Conrade.

CONRADE

What the goodyear, my lord! Why are you thus out of measure sad?

DON JOHN

There is no measure in the occasion that breeds, therefore the sadness is without limit.

CONRADE

You should hear reason.

DON JOHN

And when I have heard it, what blessing brings it?

CONRADE

If not a present remedy, at least a patient sufferance.

DON JOHN

I wonder that thou – being as thou sayst thou art, born under Saturn – goest about to apply a moral medicine to a mortifying mischief. I cannot hide what I am. I must be sad when I have cause, and smile at no man's jests; eat when I have stomach, and wait for no man's leisure; sleep when I am drowsy, and tend on no man's business; laugh when I am merry, and claw no man in his humour.

(1.3.1–17)

What we have learned so far is only that Don John was an opponent of his brother in the wars from which the siblings are returning, but that allegedly they are now reconciled. In the passage quoted above, Don John introduces himself to us as a character who is morose, sullen and defines himself as an outsider, seething with discontent. He is, in other words, a classic 'malcontent', a stock figure in Renaissance drama. 'Sad' in early modern English did not just mean gloomy, as today, but serious and solemn. Even though he evokes the planet Saturn to refer to its influence over his companion, the resonances of the reference to Saturn linger to shape our view of the speaker himself. Saturn was the star associated with the humour called black bile, an excess of which was thought to cause melancholy. In the Galenic physiology that dominated medical thought from antiquity until the Renaissance, astrology, medicine and psychology were all closely intertwined with each other in ways that are difficult for us to unravel today. This conglomeration of beliefs was being challenged from various sides with the proliferation of new scientific discoveries about the human body and the planetary system, but writers still found them useful as metaphorical ways of describing characters. Melancholy was a fashionable disease at this time, and striking a melancholy pose was something young men in particular were accused of. It was also the subject of deep interest – the scholar Robert Burton's weighty tome *The Anatomy of Melancholy*, first published in 1621, testifies to the immense fascination that the topic exerted. Today we assume that melancholy refers mainly to a sad wistfulness, but in Galenic medicine things were more complex. The four humours that circulated in the human body, blood, phlegm, yellow bile (or choler) and black bile, were endlessly interchangeable. Confusingly, the word 'blood' was used both for one specific humour and the entire mixture. If blood was overheated, a specific humour might turn into something else, as in the case of anger – excessive heat in the body would turn yellow bile to a particularly strong form of black bile, or 'melancholy adust'. This meant that melancholy could also involve anger, or malice, or rapid mood swings between fury and misery (Hoeniger 1992: 162–78). Hamlet is a textbook case of someone affected by 'melancholy adust'. Don John, too, seems to be not simply mournful, but smouldering with rage. Only much later in the play do we learn that he is the illegitimate brother of the Prince of Aragon, Don Pedro, when Benedick refers to him as 'John the bastard' (4.1.188). At a deeper level than simple one-to-one causality, Don John might actually have a motive that goads him to harm others, one that ties up with some of the themes underlying the play: honour and social prestige, and its loss.

Don John declares himself to be different from all the other inhabitants of the play. He claims that he is transparent in his feelings: 'I cannot hide what I am' (1.3.12–13). When he is feeling gloomy, he cannot put on a social mask to laugh politely at other people's jokes; on the other hand, when he is merry, he will not conceal his amusement in order to flatter (or 'claw') others and adapt to their moods. His authenticity seems to set him apart from all the other characters, who indulge in elaborate performances of social masquerade and defer to codes of civility. As the play proceeds, we realize that Don John is grossly misrepresenting himself. Not only is he the chief engineer of one of the most cunning intrigues perpetrated on the denizens of the playworld, but he proves himself to be quite as adept at disguising his thoughts as the other characters. A clue is provided as early as in the first act – and this is precisely where a close look at the language reveals layers of meaning that we might miss if we focus on the action of the play alone. Don John describes his allegedly authentic character in lines of sophisticated diction. He uses *alliteration* ('a moral medicine to a mortifying mischief') and *metaphor* (a 'mortifying mischief' is a mortal disease, but he is also alluding to the fatal political blow that he has apparently suffered in the recent wars, in which he sided against the forces of his brother). He is at pains to stress his antisocial nature – when he is hungry or tired, he states categorically, he is not willing to adapt to the social mores of communal life – but ironically, he expresses himself in a highly polished style of language, that medium of social communication. Every single line cited in the passage above demonstrates his virtuosity in subtle speech. His prose consists of a series of balanced clauses. Take, for instance, the long last sentence, in which he repeats the same basic pattern of 'I must ... when I ...'. Many members of Shakespeare's audience would have been familiar with the rhetorical devices he is using, *parallelism*, i.e. symmetrically constructed sentences, and *zeugma*, which consists of having one word or term implicitly governing the following clauses, although it is not repeated. Don John spells out the entire phrase 'I must' only once, but it is clear that the following clauses are dominated by these two words.

His string of examples opens and closes neatly with similar ideas, which themselves are set in opposition to terms that radically invert their connotations. In effect, he is saying that when he is moody he cannot laugh at other people's jokes, and when he feels like laughing he cannot make allowance for other people's moods. He produces a complex example of what is known as *chiasmus*, a rhetorical figure in which concepts are repeated in reverse order, forming a pattern of A–B–B–A. Within the clauses bookended by the chiasmus, he deploys *antonyms* (sadness as opposed to gaiety, eating as opposed to delaying a meal, sleeping as opposed to attending to others), or a form known as *antithesis*, which is a term used for sentences built around contrasting concepts. If we return to the opening lines of the dialogue, we will note that they are no less artful. The sentence 'There is no measure in the occasion that breeds, therefore sadness is without limit' (3–4) is reminiscent of a chiasmus; 'measure' and 'limit' are virtual synonyms; 'the occasion that breeds' his sadness is, as he goes on to tell us, his sadness itself, or his melancholic personality. The line 'And when I have heard it, what blessing brings it?' (6–7) contains a symmetrical arrangement of both clauses ('heard it', 'brings it') in addition to an alliteration ('blessing', 'bring'). In his mode of speech, Don John shows himself to be as adroit in utilizing language as is the courtly set around his brother whom he so despises. His avowedly authentic personality is expressed in words that are every bit as studied as those of his polished opponents.

In his next few lines, Don John launches into even more intricate verbal pirouettes. 'I had rather be a canker in a hedge than a rose in his grace, and it better fits my blood to be disdained of all than to fashion a carriage to rob love from any', he asserts (1.3.25–7). What he seems to be saying is that he would prefer to resemble a flower growing wild than the more valuable and prestigious rose; he would prefer his freedom to being a decorative courtier in the good graces of his brother, Don Pedro. It suits him better to be despised than to adopt a form of behaviour that would ingratiate him with others. Once again, he is insisting on his dogged independence and wilful, unsociable nature. The image he uses is taken from flora – 'canker' was a name for a wild rose or dog rose, a shrub that grows wild and was often contrasted to roses cultivated in gardens, traditionally regarded as the most choice of all flowers. But Don John's declaration carries an implicit threat. The term 'canker' could also refer to a cankerworm, a parasite that attacked plants and insidiously destroyed their most beautiful and most vulnerable parts, flowers. 'Canker' could, in fact, be applied to any form of disease that ate up the object it invaded from the inside, like a cancer. In these lines, Don John is delivering his credo: his mission is to demolish all that is generally considered beautiful and graceful. The term 'grace' has connotations not only of courtly style, but of the term used to address a ruler, and plays on the floral metaphor, with a *pun* on 'grass'. A further implicit irony lies in the fact that the canker rose was in fact a common device in heraldry, and an emblem of legitimate noble birth. Don John uses a second pun on the word 'blood', which could refer to his humour as well as to his illegitimate birth and degraded status – a state he implicitly calls into question with the image of the canker rose.

Once again, there is a strict symmetry in the two lines. The words 'I had rather be' is repeated in alternative form in the words 'it better fits my blood'; the image of the canker is equated with being disdained by everyone; the image of the rose is paired with the notion of adopting a demeanour to gain favour. But the language he actually uses is anything but straightforward. To 'fashion a carriage' carries the connotations of artificial behaviour, something that Don John once again attributes to the courtiers surrounding his brother and that he presents as contrary to his own unpretentious conduct. The term 'fashion' will emerge as one of the keywords of the entire play – here, it is repeated for the third time, within the very first act. The first mention of 'fashion' is in Scene 1, when Beatrice mocks Benedick as addicted to the latest sartorial fads, remarking caustically, 'He wears his faith but as the fashion of his hat: it ever changes with the next block' (1.1.70–2). A block was a mould dressmakers used to shape hats. Beatrice is also implicitly making a thrust at Benedick's lack of constancy – her comment gains relevance in the light of later developments in the relationship between the two verbal fencers. When Don Pedro greets Leonato, he says with impeccable politeness, 'The fashion of the world is to avoid cost, and you encounter it' (1.1.92). Imagery taken from fashion is used in a flamboyant speech by Benedick, when he mocks the forays into the realm of wit by his boon companions, Claudio and Don Pedro. 'The body of your discourse is sometime guarded with fragments, and the guards are but slightly basted on neither' (1.1.266–8), he scoffs. Terms such as 'guards' and 'basted' are borrowed from the idiom of tailoring: a 'guard' was a trimming and 'to baste' meant to sew on loosely. Benedick is using a rather fanciful metaphor from the world of fashion to jeer at the efforts of his friends to adopt a modish form of speech, namely wit. The frills and flounces with which they are trying to decorate their attempts at wit are merely borrowed scraps (read: clichés). In addition, these are so precariously attached that they might fall off any minute. Before the action has got into its stride, references to fashion are liberally strewn in the conversation. In the most famous passage on fashion, discussed in Chapter 2, the conceit of fashion as a thief will be elaborated on extensively – something hinted at in the strange phrase 'to rob love'. Here it implies that the courtiers who are busy setting themselves out in the best possible light to cut a good figure at court are in fact insinuating themselves into princely favour under false pretences. Their attractiveness is merely a façade – they do not really deserve the preferential treatment that they will secure by means of their stylish behaviour.

The changes Shakespeare makes to his source material are often well worth pursuing. Why might Shakespeare have dropped the explicit motive for his villain to harm the lovers and besmirch Hero's integrity? The reason might lie partly in what generations of spectators and readers have pinned down as one of the most memorable aspects of his works: characters who seem to be made of flesh and blood. Shakespeare's mastery of inserting little touches to bring the people who throng his plays to life is one reason why these texts have endured for so many centuries, and surely one typical device is the opacity he deliberately invokes as far as the motivation of the characters is concerned. This confirms our own knowledge of human nature – the fact that in real-life people are not as clear cut as in fiction, that reasons why we do something are often many-facetted, that sometimes we ourselves are unaware of what deeper impulses might have spurred us, or those we live with, to undertake a certain course of action, or to fail to do so. In other words, one of the hallmarks of Shakespeare's art is the fact that the plays delve into realms of the human unconscious and reveal a depth of psychological insight into their characters.

In the case of *Much Ado About Nothing*, other considerations might also have played a role. When Don John says 'it better fits my blood to be disdained of all' (1.3.26–7), he is using the word 'blood' in a highly ambivalent way. In terms of humoral physiology, in which blood consisted of a mixture of humours, the proportion of which was decisive in determining a person's moods and, by extension, personality, the remark alludes to Don John's dark, saturnine character. In characteristically perverse manner, he prefers to be an outcast instead of attempting to inveigle his way into the affection of his brother (or anyone else, for that matter). But the remark might also hint at Don John's birth and the fact that he is a bastard. With heavy irony, he comments on the stereotype of a bastard, which in a hierarchical society involved a lack of the attributes associated with those of aristocratic descent – moral qualities superior to those of the rest of humanity. In a social world rigidly divided by rank, the well-born were assumed to possess virtues such as a distinctive sense of honour, magnanimity, wisdom and courage simply by dint of their noble birth. An aristocrat of illegitimate origin was not merely a source of shame. He or she was deemed to be innately flawed, inclined by nature towards evil. The play removes the motivation of the villain as rooted in jealous rivalry only to replace it with a suggestion that the shame and dishonour inflicted on Don John might be one factor that has incited him to take revenge on the closest companion of Don Pedro, whose legitimate status has endowed him with the right to rule over his brother. At one stroke, the change Shakespeare makes to the original story reinforces the shift of focus from sexual jealousy to larger questions of honour and dishonour.

A further effect of the removal of sexual rivalry as a rationale for Don John's intrigue is the light it sheds on Claudio. Shakespeare seems to go to great lengths to make his protagonist a distinctly unattractive figure. In his play, there is no rival to feed the young Count's insecurity about Hero's affections. Instead, we see a character only too willing to leap to conclusions about the unfaithfulness of his fiancée, condemning her even before he has seen the flimsy evidence that Don John fabricates. Significantly, after hearing Don John's slander, he immediately starts planning a vicious public humiliation for Hero. The church scene is one of breath-taking rhetorical violence in which Claudio maliciously goes through the initial motions of the marriage ritual only to shatter the ceremony with brutal finality, rejecting his bride straight after she has been given away by her father with the shocking words, 'Give not this rotten orange to your friend' (4.1.30). Oranges were sometimes conflated with the golden apples of ancient mythology, fruit that featured in numerous myths and symbolized sensual pleasures, particularly sexual love. An exotic and valuable commodity in the Renaissance, they were prized as emblems of a lifestyle of luxury and abundance. Alternatively, the sexual symbolism of oranges led to their being associated with prostitutes, who often doubled as fruit-sellers. What Claudio is implying that under her attractive appearance Hero hides a corrupt interior, a theme that he expatiates on at length in his following speeches. He accuses Hero of being only 'the sign and semblance of her honour' (4.1.31), using falsehood to conceal her inner deceitfulness. *Much Ado About Nothing* is built around the discrepancy between illusion and truth, between façade and reality, and how initial impressions can be manipulated for deceptive purposes. By making Claudio a callow young man whose beliefs are swayed by hearsay and surface appearances, Shakespeare foregrounds these themes, and allows the words and actions of divergent characters to echo each other in endless refractions.

In this connection, it is of central importance that the falsified proof of Hero's infidelity, the miniature drama staged by Borachio and Margaret at the window of her room in which Margaret takes on the role of Hero embracing another lover, is never staged in the play. The sources Shakespeare draws on are mainly narrative texts, so the absence of the window scene is a decision shaped by dramaturgical considerations. Many later performances actually reinsert the window scene as a mimed performance and allow the audience to view the show that Claudio and Don Pedro have watched, by means of which they have been duped. In the playtext, however, we only learn about the staged deception from Borachio before the event, when he suggests the idea to Don John (2.2), and after the event, when Borachio boasts of his deed to Conrade (3.3). What might the effect be of not staging Don John's plot? This is a question well worth examining, though here we can only deal with it briefly. It is certainly striking that in a play awash with disinformation and misinterpretation, in regard to the window show the audience too is at the receiving end of hearsay, insinuation and gossip. As with Claudio's susceptibility to malicious rumour, the decision to have the masquerade of Margaret and Borachio reported, not witnessed, reinforces the vexed issue of the relation of appearances and the truth. In addition, it works to allow the audience to step back from the action for a minute and watch the characters as they respond to the performance with a far more detached stance than might have been the case if we had been in the same situation as they were. Detachment from onstage events always enables a certain critical distance on the part of the spectators and allows us to reflect on the way the plot is unfolding in more judicious ways than if we had been caught up in the action ourselves. This critical dissociation from the characters also has an impact on the notion of shame and honour, the cultural code that no one in the play embodies more rigidly than Claudio. Presenting the window show as a non-event suggests that perhaps the entire mythology of honour to which so many of the characters are committed might be illusory – an inflated ideology with little substance.

Shakespeare's most famous addition to his sources is the invention of Beatrice and Benedick. One of the most attractive pair of lovers in Shakespeare's entire oeuvre, they have delighted generations of viewers and audiences. Far more memorable than the lovers of the main plot, Claudio and Hero, they have left their mark on the play to such an extent that it was frequently referred to with their names. They are eloquent, independent-minded, individualistic, rounded figures to whom we warm, and whose quarrels and reconciliations we follow with bated breath and passionate engagement. Apart from providing pleasure for the audience, they fulfil important functions in the play. For one thing, their relationship serves to throw the stiff, conventional alliance between Claudio and Hero into relief. The engagement of the latter couple breaks down because Claudio believes that Hero has lost her honour by entertaining relations with another man on the eve of her wedding. The assumption that a woman's honour is defined primarily through her chastity is shared by all the citizens of Messina and reflects early modern social norms. Male honour, on the other hand, was bound up with the chastity of the female members of a family, either by birth or by marriage. Jokes that circulate within a society often reflect anxieties about key values and serve to defuse them. The play is peppered with jokes about cuckoldry and how men lose face because their wives are unfaithful. Claudio claims he has been dishonoured through Hero's deeds; the Prince claims he has been dishonoured by arranging for the alliance; Leonato claims he has been dishonoured by his daughter's misconduct.

The cultural rules defining the way women were to comport themselves in society may be summed up in three words: they were to be chaste, silent and obedient. These terms were intimately connected: loquaciousness on the part of a woman tarred her with the brush of sexually licentious behaviour. The suggestion that Hero was supposedly talking to a man outside her window was sufficient proof to damn her for a lack of chastity.

The most striking thing about Beatrice is that she is one of the most articulate comic characters Shakespeare has created. Her verbal dexterity and her mastery of the cut and thrust of repartee put her in a category of her own, and certainly allow her to demolish with ease all the male contenders for the prize of wittiest person in Messina. In an earlier play, *The Taming of the Shrew*, the sharp-tongued Katherine was labelled a shrew, and, despite possibly evoking the spectators' pleasure in her bold rebellion against social mores, was tamed at the end of the play. Beatrice promises to tame her 'wild heart' (3.1.112), but there is little sign of her changing her character even after she and Benedick have become a couple. Most importantly, there is no hint that anyone in Messina considers her to be unchaste, despite her freedom in saying what she thinks. The reluctant pair of lovers, Beatrice and Benedick, provide a foil against which the relationship of the protagonists of the main plot may be gauged – and one that sheds a sceptical light on the obsession with honour they display. The way Renaissance society defined the desirable woman, and the normative equation of women's speech with their sexuality, are subtly interrogated.

If Benedick and Beatrice hold up a mirror to Claudio and Hero in terms of sexual mores, they are also closely connected to them by other central themes of the play – the roles of appearances and reality. Like the main characters, Benedick and Beatrice are victims of deception, in their case the plot thought up by the Prince to gull them into falling in love with each other. The play is careful to point up the parallels between the conspiracy of Don John and the benign strategem

of Don Pedro – parallels that, as we shall see later, are repli-
cated in the structure of the play. In its probing of the issue
of illusion, the subplot of *Much Ado About Nothing* seems to
suggest a variation on the ideas addressed in the main plot.
To what extent does deception only work in conjunction with
self-deception – and then turn into reality? Might it be the
case that Beatrice and Benedick fall in love with each other
because they want to believe that the other is in love with
them? These thoughts, powerfully explored in the play, spill
over to encompass the very medium in which the story is
presented – the theatre. The theatre is, after all, the result of
wilful illusion on the part of all those involved in creating a
performance, including the audience, who are willing to give
themselves over to the illusory world presented to them.

Lastly, a noteworthy addition to the play is the comic cast
of Dogberry and co. Shakespeare's comic subplots often reflect
the preoccupations of the play, but refracted as in a distorting
mirror. In a play preoccupied with language, and with the
power of words to destroy lives and to build relationships, the
clowns provide hilarity by displaying a bumbling, inept use
of language that misses the mark entirely. Ironically enough,
the pompous constable and the members of his watch are the
agents of unravelling the machinations of the villains, even
though they themselves have no idea of the import of what
they have witnessed and that they transmit to their betters.
Misunderstanding is, however, not a privilege of members
of the lower social orders. In this play, the self-importance
of office bearers, however humble in rank, provides comic
copy. In later plays, such as the 'problem play' *Measure for
Measure*, abuse of office was treated far more seriously, and in
King Lear, in which a king misuses his power, the dethroned
Lear jeers at the power of authority to corrupt and debase
with withering sarcasm: 'Thou hast seen a farmer's dog bark
at a beggar?' he asks, concluding, 'there thou might behold the
great image of authority: a dog's obeyed in office' (4.6.150–5).
In *Much Ado About Nothing*, the clowns are harmless
bunglers whose obsequious demeanour and bizarre speech

is mocked, but not shown as a threat, or only with a hint of what power might do to those in positions of control. With their mutilation of language, however, the comic constables contribute yet another layer to the enquiry into language that the play presents.

CHAPTER ONE

Language in context

Setting

Much Ado About Nothing opens at the residence of Leonato, the governor of Messina. This information is something readers of the play today would take for granted – they would simply consult the cast of characters and the note specifying location given at the beginning of each scene in modern editions of the play. However, these additions to the text were made over 100 years after the play was first published in a cheap edition in 1600, in a version called the First Quarto or Q1. (The *quarto* was a printing format in which sheets were folded twice to produce four leaves or eight pages.) Nor was the cast of characters and location included in the first edition of Shakespeare's collected works, the First Folio, published seven years after his death in 1616 by John Heminges and Henry Condell, his friends and fellow actors in the King's Men company. The term *folio* referred to its large size – a folio was a prestigious volume, far more expensive than a quarto. The eighteenth century was the great age of Shakespeare editions: Nicholas Rowe brought out a six-volume edition of collected works in 1709, and Alexander Pope a prestigious new edition in 1723–5. It was Rowe who introduced a list of *dramatis personae* as well as a host of stage directions. Pope inserted a note about locations, and editors have continued to do so ever since.

In the theatre in Shakespeare's age, locations were far more conjectural. For one thing, backdrops were virtually non-existent, although hangings and painted cloths were used. Some scholars assume that actors briefly appeared onstage holding up a placard with the name of the location. Although lavish costumes were part of the show, they would not have offered clues as to where and when the play was set. Unfortunately, we do not actually know much about what productions looked like on the early modern stage. The one sketch that has survived, purporting to be by the writer Henry Peacham, might well be a forgery. It depicts a scene from the early Shakespearean tragedy *Titus Andronicus*. What we see is a group of figures dressed in a motley mixture of fashions. Although the play is a Roman history, many of the characters wear articles of clothing in Elizabethan style. Theatre costumes, in other words, were clothes.

A mine of information on staging practices of Shakespeare's time is the diary of Philip Henslowe, a theatrical entrepreneur who owned several theatres and financed the acting company The Admiral's Men, the chief rival to Shakespeare's Lord Chamberlain's Men (later called the King's Men). Henslowe's 'diary' is actually a list of expenses and investments that he made in connection with his business interests in the entertainment industry. Theatre historians have found it invaluable for its insights into the running of the theatres in this period. It emerges that the largest investment by far was the acquisition of costumes, which were often the cast-off attire of noblemen. Since so many of the characters presented on stage were kings or aristocrats, sumptuous apparel was in great demand. At the same time, there was a huge turnover in second-hand clothes in London – fashions changed at such a dizzying rate, and clothes were such exorbitant items, that many noblemen were willing to dispose of their clothes to dealers in second-hand garb before reinvesting in a new set. Critics Ann Rosalind Jones and Peter Stallybrass suggest that Henslowe, who turned everything to money, might have been involved in the second-hand clothes trade too, recycling garments to other buyers apart from theatre companies (2000: 175–206). Spectators at a performance of *Much Ado About Nothing* might not have drawn conclusions about the specifically Sicilian location of the play from what the actors on stage were wearing, but they would have immediately grasped that the play was set in a world of fashionable, high-born people.

Most of the necessary background information that a play-goer would require would be transmitted through the language of the play. In the very first line, Leonato says, 'I learn in this letter that Don Pedro of Aragon comes this night to Messina' (1.1.1–2). Most members of the audience would not have a first-hand acquaintance with Italy, but they might well have been aware of the fact that for the entire sixteenth century Italy had been a plaything of the great European powers, France and Spain. Some of them might have known that Sicily had been governed by Spanish rulers for centuries, first by sovereigns of Aragon and then as part of the Habsburg Spanish empire. Shakespeare frequently used Italian settings, which exercised a significant influence on the atmosphere of many of his plays, not only the comedies. The English were fascinated by Italy. For Elizabethans, Italy, the wellspring of the Renaissance, conjured up a place steeped in art and learning, overflowing with aesthetic pleasures and exciting new ideas. It was the model of a cultivated lifestyle. At the same time, Italy was viewed with deep suspicion. It was the home of the papacy, regarded as an enemy ever since Pope Pius V issued a bull in 1570 declaring their queen to be a heretic and in effect absolving all crimes against her from the taint of sin. The impact of this declaration was enormous. It inspired a paranoia against Catholicism at the heart of the government, where the conviction grew that Catholic subjects were incessantly hatching plots against the monarch. Radical Protestants saw Italy as a hotbed of vice, in particular idolatry. The scholar Roger Ascham in his book *The Schoolmaster* (1570) cited the proverb 'The Italianate Englishman is a devil incarnate' as a warning against young Englishmen travelling to Italy and returning with their morals corrupted (66). As he concedes, this was originally an Italian proverb that contained a warning against Englishmen in Italy, perhaps inspired by the ruthless fourteenth-century mercenary Sir John Hawkwood. It is included in the collection of Italian proverbs published in 1591 by the Italian immigrant to England John Florio in his language manual *Florio's Second Frutes*. Florio, who sardonically described himself as 'an Englishman in Italiane' (sig. *1ʳ), later became famous for his translation of Montaigne's essays into English. A widespread fear was that impressionable young Englishmen would be seduced by the sensuous attractions of Roman Catholicism, with its ornate churches and rich ceremonies, and would succumb to the lure of the Catholic Church.

These were some of the reverberations that would be set off by announcing that a play was set in Italy. Italian literature was also a copious source of stories for English playwrights to exploit and was valued for its abundance of sensational plots, brimming with desire, passion, jealousy and intrigue. All these elements play a part in *Much Ado About Nothing*, and hot-blooded Italian noblemen pursuing issues of honour were a staple of English drama. Perhaps of greatest interest in this play are the echoes of the Italian culture of courtesy that it evokes. The world of the play is soaked in an exquisitely cultivated style of behaviour, one that was primarily associated with Baldassare Castiglione's landmark *Il Cortegiano*, first published in 1528. This was 'Englished' by Sir Thomas Hoby with the title *The Book of the Courtier* in 1561. Set in 1507 in the little town of Urbino on the slopes of the Apennines, Castiglione's book depicts a glittering group of noblemen, poets, musicians and artists who gather every evening in the chambers of the Duchess of Urbino, Elisabetta Gonzaga, and while away the time with jests, pleasantries and artful parlour games. The book turns on one of these games, in which the members of the circle take turns in defining the ideal courtier. The conversations they carry on are reproduced in the text in a tantalizingly realistic manner; although the book is a work of fiction, it uses real-life characters and events to frame the dialogues, and teases the reader with the suggestion that it is simply a transcription of what really happened during four evenings in Urbino in the early sixteenth century. Castiglione was not the first to invent this literary style. The genre of the dialogue harks back to antiquity and was most famously used by Plato to present the ideas of Socrates. Castiglione's direct model was Cicero, whose *De Oratore* [*On the Ideal Orator*] was written in 55 BC, but purportedly took place some decades earlier. Cicero's dialogue is situated in the bucolic surroundings of a country villa in Tusculum and features speakers who were real people, although they were all dead by the time Cicero wrote his work. Cicero's text is about the art of rhetoric and the skills orators should acquire, a topic we will turn to in Chapter 2. Castiglione's dialogue is about the accomplishments the ideal courtier should attain, which included the art of conversation. In *Much Ado About Nothing*, we observe how courtly characters indulge in banter, jokes and skirmishes of wit, but at its best their language is anything but ornate and stilted. Beatrice and Benedick still delight audiences today precisely because their speech sparkles with vivacity and verve.

Castiglione's ideas were diffused throughout Europe. A century after its publication, 125 editions had appeared, about sixty of them in translation (Burke 1995: 158–62). *The Book of the Courtier* precipitated a flurry of other books of courtesy in the print marketplace. Ironically, what was originally intended as a treatise to defend the role of the nobility was avidly read as a how-to manual for social climbers (Whigham 1984). In England, Castiglione's influence in courtly circles was pervasive. It is not clear whether Shakespeare ever read *The Courtier*, but perhaps the question is not as relevant as it might appear. In a study of what works Shakespeare might have read, Robert Miola writes:

> The old model of creativity was vertical and hierarchical with the author in the middle: Shakespeare read books and transformed them into works of art; subtexts lay beneath

the texts of his work. The new model is horizontal and associative; texts all exist in complicated cultural relations to each other. According to some critics these days, there are no source texts, only an endless and bewitching array of intertexts. (2000: 169)

What Miola is arguing is that, from a contemporary viewpoint, whether or not Shakespeare used *The Book of the Courtier* as inspiration for his play is not decisive. Castiglione's book was highly influential in the Renaissance and had been circulating in the public sphere for much of the sixteenth century. Texts affect each other in subtle, varied ways. *The Courtier* gained iconic status for readers interested in matters of graceful social interaction. Early modern society was one that was obsessed with status and the aspiration to climb up the social ladder. Shakespeare and his fellow playwrights recognized that spectators were keen to watch aristocrats at close range and to pick up elite forms of deportment from the dashing characters presented to them on stage. Perhaps a model of fashionable behaviour was one of the products that they retailed in the early modern market for entertainment (Dawson and Yachnin 2001). What *Much Ado About Nothing* shares with Castiglione's *Book of the Courtier* is not only a dazzling display of wit, but a self-awareness about its own status as a fictive product that was involved in marketing its own stylishness.

Style and grace

Unlike the *Book of the Courtier*, *Much Ado About Nothing* is not set at court, but the residents of Messina clearly aspire to the status of courtly life. This becomes clear in the opening exchange between Leonato and the messenger, both from what they say and from how they speak. Take, for instance, the very first snippet of conversation:

LEONATO
How many gentlemen have you lost in this action?
MESSENGER
But few of any sort, and none of name.
LEONATO
A victory is twice itself when the achiever brings home
full numbers. I find here that young Don Pedro hath
bestowed much honour on a young Florentine called
Claudio.

(1.1.5–11)

Leonato is entirely concerned with the noblemen involved
in the war – the word 'gentlemen' was a generic term for
all degrees of nobility as well as the name for one specific
rank, the lowest rung of the well-born (Kelso 1964). In a
society stratified by hierarchy, it was customary to distinguish
between the blue-blooded casualties of warfare and, as the
messenger puts it, those 'of name' and other ranks – the best
and the rest. But Leonato's exclusive focus on the former is
subtly underscored by his comment about 'full numbers',
casually ignoring the messenger's reference to a small number
of lost soldiers. His next remark shows his eagerness to discuss
important aristocratic personages in the train of the Prince,
such as Claudio. A stock feature of comic plots is the necessity
for young lovers to overcome obstacles to their union, one
of the chief being disapproving fathers. This plot device was
something English playwrights borrowed from Roman plays
by Plautus and Terence, who for their part adopted ideas from
the Greek 'new comedy' of Menander. The lovers were often
aided by a witty slave, who was the cleverest person on stage.
In *Much Ado About Nothing* Shakespeare ironically depicts a
father only too eager to marry off his daughter to her suitor.
Indeed, his snobbery is such that he is keen to angle for the
biggest prize available on the marriage market, with his hopes
briefly set on the Prince himself. When his brother excitedly
passes on the (mistaken) rumour about the Prince's intentions

with regard to Hero, he labels it 'a dream' (1.2.18). But he is quick to settle for the next best option, the Count Claudio.

Social pretensions are not the prerogative of Leonato, however. The messenger speaks in a mannered, highly patterned prose style that at least some members of the audience would immediately associate with the courtly style of euphuism, a style that flourished in the 1580s at the Elizabethan court and took its name from the prose romances by the writer John Lyly, *Euphues: The Anatomy of Wit* (1578) and *Euphues and his England* (1580). Trademark characteristics of this manner of speech were balanced clauses, antitheses, a wealth of alliteration and rhetorical questions. Shakespeare frequently mocks users of a euphuistic style, such as Polonius in *Hamlet* – in response to a particularly tedious effusion on the councillor's part, the Queen drily comments 'More matter with less art' (2.2.95). Euphuistic speakers in his plays are often characters who move in court circles, but who are not quite from the top drawer themselves. The messenger, a negligible character hovering on the fringes of high society, tries to attract attention with his rhetorical flourishes. Of Claudio he says, 'He hath borne himself beyond the promise of his age, doing in the figure of a lamb the feats of a lion; he hath indeed better bettered expectation than you must expect of me to tell you how' (1.1.13–16). In what might have been a simple answer to a transparent request for more information about Claudio by Leonato, he packs multiple alliterative effects ('borne', 'beyond', 'better', 'bettered'; 'figure', 'feats'; 'lamb', 'lion'; 'expectation', 'expect'), antithesis ('figure' – or face – as opposed to 'feats', 'lamb' as opposed to 'lion') and two examples of *polypton*, the rhetorical figure in which words derived from the same root are repeated in various mutations – here, 'better' and 'bettered'; 'expectation' and 'expect'. Not only is the nameless messenger trying to better his betters, as no doubt he would put it, or to outdo Leonato, who until now has been expressing himself with admirable lucidity, but his comparison of the young soldier to a lamb is ridiculous. (In an acerbic touch, only apparent after the plot has run its course, the play reveals Claudio's leonine qualities only in his violence towards his bride.) The next remark the messenger makes is even more precious. When talking about Claudio's uncle, he says, 'there appears much joy in him, even so much that joy could not show itself modest enough without a badge of bitterness' (20–2). This time his remarks come packaged in the form of a chiasmus, where 'appear' is followed by 'joy' and then a second 'joy' comes before 'show', a variation on 'appear', although he does sprinkle in alliteration ('badge', 'bitterness') for good measure. What he no doubt means to say is that the uncle was exultant to hear the good news, but for the sake of decorum or good manners he had to moderate ('modest' means moderate) the appearance of his delight and display some sign (or 'badge') of unhappiness. Significantly, in this play about surfaces and show, these trite comments do not turn on reining in one's feelings, but on the outward expression of emotion. Even at this point the play is preoccupied with decorous behaviour and social impressions.

Unsurprisingly, Leonato needs to investigate further to unpack this baffling statement. 'Did he break out in tears?' (23), the mystified governor enquires. But euphuism is infectious, and in this play characters are distinguished by how laboured or how smooth their speech is. Leonato joins the messenger in expressing himself in a convoluted manner. 'A kind overflow of kindness; there are no faces truer than those that are so washed. How much better is it to weep at joy than to joy at weeping!' (25–7). His utterance is a small attempt to gain the upper hand in the contest of modish speech. He uses a pun, playing on the word 'kind', which at the time bore a range of meanings, including a reference to natural kinship. The uncle of Claudio was overcome by emotion not only because he is a generous-spirited person and fond of his nephew, but because it would be natural reaction of someone of close kin. He wraps up his observation with a sententious *paradox* about sorrow and joy (in the form of a chiasmus: weep–joy, joy–weeping). Actually, his comment does contribute a suggestive note to the tone of the play. The term 'kind' refers not only to humane feelings and natural bonds, but also to gracious behaviour befitting the high-born. Similarly, the connotations of 'true', like 'honest', point to the nobility. As will be discussed in Chapter 3, rank in the early modern age was not merely a matter of social status – it was justified on the basis of inherent qualities that only the aristocracy were presumed to possess, which is what determined their elusive sense of 'honour'. Generosity of spirit, faithfulness to one's word, trustworthiness and constancy were virtues that were associated with those of a higher pedigree than the common people. Leonato's words remind us that honour and social standing are major concerns of the play. Leonato, the governor of Messina, might be well respected and affluent and no doubt belongs to the gentry (or lower echelons of nobility). The Prince of Aragon and the Count Claudio are players in a different league altogether. The truism about tears being an index of true feelings touches upon the overarching theme of what we can deduce from outside appearances – or not, as the case might be. What the unknown messenger and the governor of Messina share is the fact that both are, as it were, social aspirants, keen to move on equal terms with those of a higher rank. The strain of trying to do so is reflected in their speech.

Lastly, Leonato's reflection about the paradox of sorrow and joy – and it might be helpful to remind ourselves that in rhetorical terms paradox refers to a statement that appears contradictory at first sight, but that nevertheless contains a deeper truth – sounds a note of warning about the comic action of the play. As in so many of Shakespeare's comedies, the light-hearted strains of the plot are irrevocably entangled with sadness. Before the play ends, Leonato and his family will have undergone an extraordinary ordeal, the anguish of which will not quite be expunged by the happy ending. In a nice trace of irony, the play ends with a messenger, as it begins – a reminder, perhaps, that life itself does not run in grooves as smooth as the artful pattern of a play.

For those striving to attain higher social spheres, Castiglione's *Book of the Courtier* served as an indispensable guidebook. In Book 1 the chief interlocutor, Count Ludovico Canossa, outlines a catalogue of skills that the courtier should master – skills that encompass both arts and letters and range from the art of warfare, horsemanship, physical exercises such as hunting, vaulting on horseback, swimming and jumping to accomplishments in music and painting. Above all, as the Count points out, the courtier's actions should be tempered with 'a certain good judgment and grace' (1.21). When asked how exactly one could acquire this element of grace, he launches into what has probably become the most famous passage in the entire book. He proposes one universal rule: 'to avoid affectation in every way possible as though it were some very rough and dangerous reef; and (to pronounce a new word perhaps) to practice in all things a certain *sprezzatura* [nonchalance], so as to conceal all art and make whatever is done or said appear to be without effort and almost without any thought about it' (1.26). Castiglione draws on the classical idea of art that conceals art, a notion that, amongst others, Cicero discusses in connection with oratory in *Orator* and Ovid advocates in the realm of social behaviour in *Ars Amatoria*. What is crucial is to produce an appearance of effortlessness in all one says and does. By contrast, the cardinal social solecism is to show the hard work one has invested in producing a social performance. Castiglione coins a new word, *sprezzatura*, which is rooted in the Italian verb *sprezzare*, meaning to disdain or scorn, to express the idea that it was imperative to avoid any impression of exertion. This key idea lies at the heart of the programme he fashioned for the self-definition of the nobility.

Judging by their language, both Leonato and the messenger seem to be trying a little too hard to demonstrate their linguistic finesse. By contrast, Don Pedro demonstrates effortless grace and style when he greets Leonato. 'Good signor Leonato, are you come to meet your trouble? The fashion of the world is to avoid cost, and you encounter it' (1.1.91–3), he says. We later learn that Leonato will be hosting the Prince and his cohort for at least a month (142–3). In reality, the governor probably has little choice in the matter. In response to Leonato's flowery welcome speech, Don Pedro remarks, 'You embrace your charge too willingly' (98). The term 'charge' could refer to a duty or the cost it entailed. Nevertheless, the relations of power involved are concealed beneath a veneer of exquisite courtesy. He graciously compliments Hero for her similarity to her father – 'Be happy, lady, for you are like an honourable father' (105–6) – and refuses the precedence that is his due (153). His brother, the malcontent, distances himself from this world of gracious words and gestures. His rejoinder to Leonato's greeting is curt: 'I am not of many words, but I thank you' (150–1).

Wit I: Beatrice

Elegant compliments and easy small talk are only one aspect of the code of courtesy. What is just as important is to display a talent for wit and mastery of the art of repartee. The second book of *The Book of the Courtier* is devoted to a disquisition on humour and contains a cornucopia of amusing stories, many of which Castiglione lifted wholesale from Cicero's *De Oratore* and which were subsequently recycled in other manuals of courtesy. The description of the evenings of conversation in Urbino has enchanted readers with the verbal jousting between the courtiers, notably between one of the leading ladies present, Emilia Pia, and Gaspare Pallavicino, who plays the role of misogynist in chief. Critics have long argued that Beatrice and Benedick are based on these models (Scott 1901; Collington 2006). As with Emilia Pia and Pallavicino, their enmity is tempered with mutual attraction – the friction of their clashes has an erotic charge.

The messenger is clearly out of his depth when faced with Beatrice's biting wit. He is nonplussed at the nickname she attaches to Benedick, 'Signor Mountanto' (28), scoffing at his penchant for the fashionable pastime of fencing – *montanto* was a fencing term – and hinting that his skill as a soldier was more a matter of stylish moves than real ability. When the messenger defends him, remonstrating that he was 'a good soldier too, lady', Beatrice nimbly turns the words around in his mouth, retorting tartly that Benedick was 'a good soldier to a lady' (50–1). The messenger stuffily declares Benedick to be 'stuffed with all honourable virtues', only to have Beatrice once again invert the meaning of his words by agreeing that Benedick was indeed 'a stuffed man' (53–5). The messenger uses the word 'stuffed' to mean that Benedick was replete with virtues; Beatrice mockingly uses the expression 'a stuffed man' to evoke the funny and deflating image of a dummy. Leonato hastens to explain to the messenger that there was 'a kind of merry war' between the two sparring partners. Vanquished by her superior wit, the messenger is so intimidated that he takes good care to remain in Beatrice's good books: 'I will hold friends with you, lady' (86).

The pretentious messenger is not the only person in the play to witness Beatrice's quick wit in action. As with Benedick, many of her barbs are directed against the state of marriage. When Leonato indulgently warns her that she will never find a husband if she remains sharp tongued, and when her uncle Antonio adds that 'she's too curst', complaining about her peevish and irascible nature, she replies, 'Too curst is more than curst. I shall lessen God's sending that way; for it is said "God sends a curst cow short horns" – but to a cow too curst he sends none' (2.1.18–21). She takes up his reproach and, after a pun on 'too' to signify 'two', fashions an amusing mock syllogism in response, arguing that since cantankerous cows are thought to be equipped with short horns, the more cantankerous she is, the less likely she is to have any horns at all. The ingenuity of her remark lies in her sleight of hand in equating the real-life horns of a cow to the metaphorical idea of wearing horns as a symbol of cuckoldry. By being prickly and unapproachable, she seems to imply, she might escape the fate of a wife whose husband cheats on her. She seems to share a deep-seated fear of being betrayed with Benedick, whose jests incessantly circle around the theme of cuckoldry.

It is unusual to find a female character in an early modern play using the imagery of cuckoldry for herself, a sign of the assertiveness and independent-mindedness of Beatrice.

Another similarity that she shares with Benedick is that her conversation persistently turns on the theme of love. At the same time, every fibre of her being rebels at the thought of entering into marriage as a subordinate partner. Men, she argues, are fallible mortal creatures, as are women: 'Would it not grieve a woman to be overmastered with a piece of valiant dust?' (53–4). When Leonato suggests that she might like a husband who was very young and hence less domineering she brushes the suggestion aside and delivers a droll account of her ideal relationship with men.

BEATRICE
What should I do with him? Dress him in my apparel and make him my waiting-gentlewoman? He that hath a beard is more than a youth, and he that hath no beard is less than a man; and he that is more than a youth is not for me, and he that is less than a man, I am not for him. Therefore I will even take sixpence in earnest of the bearward and lead his apes into hell.
LEONATO
Well then, go you into hell?
BEATRICE
No, but to the gate, and there will the devil meet me like an old cuckold with horns on his head, and say, 'Get you to heaven, Beatrice, get you to heaven. Here's no place for you maids!' So deliver I up my apes and away to Saint Peter fore the heavens. He shows me where the bachelors sit, and there live we as merry as the day is long.

(2.1.29–43)

It appears from contemporary accounts that some Elizabethan women preferred impressionable youths to older men, a conjecture that is supported by literature of the period. A classic example is Olivia in *Twelfth Night*, who is receptive to the charms of Cesario, actually Viola in disguise, perhaps because he appears to be far more sensitive to the wishes of a woman than a self-absorbed, authoritative figure like Orsino. Young men were thought to be more malleable, and in an age when many women who were interested in marriage were mature women, often widows who were unwilling to submit to the dominance of an older man, this might seem an attractive trait. In his conduct book, *Of Domesticall Duties* (1622), the Puritan divine William Gouge castigates women who marry younger men in order to rule over them (quoted in Kelso 1956: 94). The early modern age was a time when life expectancy was far shorter than today, and some men and women married several times during their lives, even though divorce was not an option and annulment was extremely rare. Widows were often relatively young women who had not only gained sexual experience but experience in running a business or a large household as well. Legally, wives were subject to the authority of their husbands, who were entitled to any property they might have brought with them into the marriage and without whose permission they were unable to enter into any contractual relations. Widows, on the other hand, were in control of both the property and enterprises that they might have inherited from their deceased spouses (see Amussen 1988; Fletcher 1995). Early modern drama abounds with attractive young widows and penniless young men whose dream it is to capture the prize of such a woman.

Beatrice, however, finds no appeal in the idea of a younger man of whom she might be in command. She yearns for an alliance of equality. Her long speech is a fantasy of emancipation and of a collaborative relationship with men that is far ahead of her time. Playing on the word 'beard', she moves to the image of a bearward or bear-keeper, who will pay her in advance ('in earnest') to take over his job. She deftly splices together the idea of a bear-keeper with the proverbial notion that spinsters were condemned to lead apes into hell. But she turns this disparaging image on its head – instead of a punishment, in her tale it mutates into a whimsical narrative of a journey from hell into heaven, with Beatrice on affable terms with both the devil and St Peter. As she notes, the devil is depicted with horns, the same symbol traditionally associated with cuckoldry, so clearly he belongs in the long line of married people whose partners were unfaithful. Beatrice's vision of paradise is one in which she is finally able to live out a life of companionship with other unmarried men and women (the term 'bachelor' covered both). Hell was for the married.

In one of her most famous speeches, she spins out a grotesque allegory of marriage that contains a kernel of sober truth in the garb of a fanciful and highly entertaining metaphor.

> [W]ooing, wedding and repenting is as a Scotch jig, a measure and a cinque-pace. The first suit is hot and hasty, like a Scotch jig, and full as fantastical; the wedding mannerly-modest as a measure, full of state and ancientry; and then comes Repentence, and with his bad legs falls into the cinque-pace faster and faster, till he sink into his grave.
>
> (2.1.64–70)

Drawing on the imagery of dancing, Beatrice compares different stages of a marriage to different types of dance. The phase of wooing is passionate and fast paced, and the wedding itself as decorous as the traditional stately dance known as a measure. Then she shifts into a personification of repentance, portraying him as an old man whirling around frantically in a lively dance, the cinque-pace, until he sinks down (at this point she introduces a pun on the English pronunciation of 'cinque-pace') and dies of exhaustion. Her cynical depiction of the trajectory of married life, which begins with romance and ends with regret, is so acute that she elicits grudging admiration from her uncle, Leonato, who admits, 'you apprehend passing shrewdly' (71).

Unlike her uncle, Beatrice is not overawed by the presence of the Prince, and continues her stream of quips even on solemn occasions, such as the moment when Don Pedro disabuses Claudio of his impression that he was being deceived, and that the Prince was wooing Hero for himself. Beatrice makes a tart comment about the sulking Count: 'The count is neither sad, nor sick, nor merry, nor well – but civil count, civil as an orange, and something of that jealous complexion' (2.1.269–71). Her intention might be to lighten the tense mood by making a homophonic pun, playing on the similarities in sound between 'civil', which implied civility in the sense of decorous behaviour, and the Spanish city of Seville, known for its oranges, and reinforcing the pun with a string of alliterations ('neither', 'nor', 'nor'; 'sad', 'sick', 'civil'; 'count', 'complexion'). Ironically, the words take on a rather darker meaning in retrospect, foreshadowing the outburst of sexual jealousy that Claudio will soon give way to, and his savage sabotage of the wedding ceremony, delivering his notorious analogy between Hero and a 'rotten orange' (4.1.30). The Count might possess the trappings of courtesy, but his cultured exterior is only skin deep. When the misunderstanding is cleared up, and the Count is given Hero's hand in marriage, Beatrice encourages the tongue-tied Claudio with a facetious remark: 'Speak, Count, 'tis your cue' (2.1.280). The gag is directed as much to the audience as to the characters present, this time not by prefiguring future developments in the narrative, but by breaking the illusion of the playworld entirely. Of course, this is precisely what the actor playing Claudio would be doing – waiting for his cue to deliver his lines. Theatre historians Simon Palfrey and Tiffany Stern have revolutionized the way we see early modern theatrical practice, and have revealed that actors were not given the entire play to read, but only their own roles. The early modern theatre had a large turnover of plays due to the relatively small size of the play-going population in London at the time, the central position of the theatre in the market for entertainment and the sharp competition between rival playhouses. New plays were staged every couple of weeks, which meant that play runs were few and players under constant pressure to learn new

roles. In this context, cues took on a far greater significance
for actors than in the theatre today. The joke embedded in
the metatheatrical jest that Beatrice is making is the fact that
the line she delivers is, in effect, the cue for the actor playing
Claudio. As will be discussed in Chapter 3, the play abounds
in metatheatrical allusions, not all of them comic.

Don Pedro is so taken with Beatrice's wit that he makes her
a half-serious marriage proposal: 'Will you have me, lady?'
Beatrice responds with a mocking reply, which bears a hint
of sauciness: 'No, my lord, unless I might have another for
working days. Your grace is too costly to wear every day'
(2.1.300–3). Laughingly, she suggests that one Prince is not
sufficient for her – she requires two of his kind. She packages
her rebuff in a compliment, metaphorically comparing Don
Pedro to an expensive garment and claiming he is too precious
to wear in everyday life. In point of fact, Beatrice is by no
means an appropriate match for a prince, and she reveals
her good sense by admitting as much. Nevertheless, no other
character in the play would have been capable of speaking to
the Prince in such a manner. No other character, that is, except
Benedick.

Wit II: Benedick

The play has become famous most of all for the fireworks of
wit that erupt when both antagonists are on stage together.
Beatrice insults Benedick during the masque by labelling him
'the prince's jester' (2.1.125), while she is mortified to hear
him compare her biting humour to the stale jokes of the moth-
eaten jestbook, *The Hundred Merry Tales* (117–18). In truth,
they are remarkably similar. Both play the roles of licensed
fools in their society, permitted to speak truths that others
avoid. Both break with the conventions of their peers, Beatrice
through her free-spirited attitude towards the other sex and
Benedick by undermining the united front of the male world

against Hero. In terms of their wit, however, there are differences between them. As so often in Shakespeare's comedies, where the women tend to be sprightlier and cleverer than the men, Beatrice's brand of humour is by far superior. Benedick's jokes turn mainly on the perennial theme of cuckoldry and serve chiefly to cement the bonds between the smart young men of the play: Claudio, Don Pedro and Benedick. His worth is measured by his entertainment value – the Prince plans to take him along on his travels, 'for from the crown of his head to the sole of his foot, he is all mirth' (3.2.8–9). Once he turns against his clique and makes a courageous stand in support of Hero, he is no longer considered amusing.

Like Leonato and the messenger, Benedick speaks in a highly symmetrical prose, but in contrast to them he gives his lines a jocular spin and spices them with the occasional extravagant quirk of fantasy. When Claudio asks for his opinion about Hero, he replies, 'Why, i'faith methinks she's too low for a high praise, too brown for a fair praise and too little for a great praise. Only this commendation can I afford her: that were she other than she is, she were unhandsome; and being no other but as she is, I do not like her' (1.1.163–7). The echoes of a euphuistic style are apparent, for instance in the parallelism of the lines, which follow a similar structure. The first three clauses consist of adjectives and qualifiers ('too low', 'too brown', 'too little') followed by a series of repeated, if varied, phrases ('a high praise', 'a fair praise', 'a great praise'). In addition, the sentence abounds in antitheses, with 'low' set against 'high', 'brown' against 'fair' and 'little' against 'great'. The regular pattern continues in the next line, where the clauses 'were she other than she is' and 'being no other but as she is' closely resemble each other. The comical surprise effect comes from the convoluted way in which Benedick grudgingly admits that Hero is beautiful, with a tortuous double negation (saying, in effect, were she not as she is, she would not be attractive), only to wind up stating flatly that she is not to his taste. It is no wonder that Claudio does not know what exactly he means.

For Benedick, the matter is clear. It is irrelevant how attractive or not Hero might be. He is appalled at the thought that one of his friends will desert their coterie to get married. 'Is't come to this?' he exclaims in mock-horror. He expresses his exasperation with Claudio in a string of rhetorical questions. 'In faith, hath not the world one man but he will wear his cap with suspicion? Shall I never see a bachelor of threescore again? Go to, i'faith. An thou wilt needs thrust thy neck into a yoke, and wear the print of it and sigh away Sundays' (186–90). The grotesque image about wearing a cap with 'suspicion' (which at the time meant anxiety) is an allusion to the metaphorical horns associated with cuckoldry. A cuckold would anxiously attempt to cover these up by donning a cap, always fearful that he might be exposed. Ludicrously, by wearing a cap he would only draw attention to himself and nurture the suspicion that he was married to an unfaithful wife. Benedick is lamenting that fact that every member of the male sex – apart from himself – is wilfully prepared to enter into servitude, which is what he sees in marriage. Like oxen, husbands are roped to their wives, forced to lead lives of plodding monotony on weekdays and sheer boredom on Sundays.

It becomes apparent that Benedick's fixation with cuckoldry is less a question of the inherent deceitfulness of women than a symptom of his abhorrence of marriage, which to him implies the end of carefree youth and male companionship. His aversion is one that ripples across early modern drama. Shakespeare's love plots, for instance, frequently grapple with the tension between male bonding and commitments to romantic partners. In *Romeo and Juliet*, Romeo is torn between his loyalties to Mercutio and to Juliet, and in *The Two Gentlemen of Verona*, the friendship of Proteus and Valentine is jeopardized through their rivalry for the love of Silvia. In *The Merchant of Venice*, Portia initiates the ring plot entirely to test her newly-wedded husband, Bassanio, and wean him away from his friend, Antonio. In *Love's Labour's Lost*, the members of the 'academe' first vow to renounce women, then undertake a policy change and set out to woo the ladies in a collaborative enterprise. And in *The Winter's Tale*, Polixenes reminisces nostalgically about his adolescent intimacy with Leontes, and implies that their fall from paradise was tied up with their newly-found interest in women. In *Much Ado About Nothing*, it is Benedick who later abandons the company of his peers, opting for allegiance to Beatrice instead.

At this stage, however, his speech chimes perfectly with that of the two higher-ranking noblemen, complementing their words with his witty remarks. The way their lines are playfully synchronized with each other reflects the amicability and comradeship between the members of the group. Take, for instance, an example from their discussion about Hero:

DON PEDRO
By my troth, I speak my thought.
CLAUDIO
And in faith, my lord, I spoke mine.
BENEDICK
And by my two faiths and troths, my lord, I spoke mine.
CLAUDIO
That I love her, I feel.
DON PEDRO
That she is worthy, I know.
BENEDICK
That I neither feel how she should be loved nor know how she should be worthy is the opinion that fire cannot melt out of; I will die in it at the stake.

(1.1.210–18)

The exchange, using the technique known as *stichomythia*, which involves single lines spoken by alternate speakers, remains unremarkable, despite its patterned structure, until Benedick adds his mite and gives it a comic slant. The device he uses is *hyperbole*, or exaggeration. In the line about 'two faiths and troth', for example, he multiplies entities that are usually spoken of in the singular. One assumes that a pledge of faith is an expression of exclusive allegiance, not a bundle of loyalties. Similarly, a trivial matter such as whether or not Hero is worthy of Claudio's love hardly warrants an oath to die as a martyr. As the conversation proceeds, Benedick increasingly ramps up his rhetoric until it reaches outrageous proportions. Never, he swears, will he fall in love. 'Prove that ever I lose more blood with love than I will get again with drinking, pick out mine eyes with a ballad-maker's pen and hang me up at the door of a brothel-house for the sign of blind Cupid', he challenges the Prince and Claudio (233–6). In early modern pathology, being in love was thought to take a toll on one's humoral balance, draining away blood from the heart. Conversely, consuming wine was believed to restore the equilibrium of humours. In a wild flight of fancy, Benedick declares that he would be willing to be blinded with the pen of a writer of love songs and then strung up as a sign outside a brothel, advertising their trade in a grotesque parody of Cupid, the blind god of Love, if ever he capitulated to love. His imagination bounds from idea to idea, leading him to give the vision of himself as a signboard a final preposterous twist: 'pluck off the bull's horns and set them in my forehead; and let me be vilely painted, and in such great letters as they write "Here is good horse to hire", let them signify under my sign, "Here you may see Benedick, the married man"' (245–9). The rhetorical device he is employing, *amplification*, involves piling on details to create a lurid image of the state the speaker is describing. All Benedick's fantasies seem to be bound up with the thought of public shaming, humiliation and losing face should he become a lover. The play itself pivots on this theme, but, ironically, it is not Benedick who is shamed – it is Hero.

Admittedly, Benedick is not seriously worried about being humbled by his friends. The main effect of his parade of cuckoldry jokes is to strengthen the ties amongst the young men. Humour frequently works to promote cohesion through affirming shared values. Jesting about the faithlessness of women and mocking other men who have submitted to female wiles and are paying the price establish a sense of solidarity among the group and work to unite them against those who don't belong. Women were fair game for jokes of this kind, given the deeply entrenched misogyny in a culture that believed women were inherently deceitful. The same mechanism is visible in other comedies. In *As You Like It*, the male protagonists sing a song celebrating cuckoldry, whose function seems to be above all to create a link between the young men in the forest of Arden. After hunting deer, they sing a song together, laughingly merging allusions to the deer's horns worn in pride by the courtier responsible for the kill with references to cuckoldry, the fate of every man.

> Take no scorn to wear the horn,
> It was a crest ere thou wast born.
> Thy father's father wore it,
> And thy father bore it.
> The horn, the horn, the lusty horn,
> Is not a thing to laugh to scorn.

$$(4.2.14–19)$$

Benedick's function in the group is to provide entertaining matter, given his talent for foolery. Despite his furious denial, his status is very similar to that of a court jester. And like Falstaff, he is not only witty in himself, but inspires wit in others. The others take great delight in gulling him into believing that Beatrice is in love with him, and strive to put on a convincing show. When he next appears, in Act 3 Scene 2, the Prince and Claudio, joined by Leonato, tease him unmercifully about being in love. They gleefully discuss the news that he has been to the barber's and seems to take pains over his appearance, relishing the opportunity to turn the tables and for once make him the butt of their jokes. All this chaffing of Benedick is in good spirits and contributes to a perennial source of humour in early modern comedy, namely fun at the expense of lovers, who were thought to be afflicted with a benign form of madness. It is only when the mood of the play darkens, after the denunciation of Hero, that the attempts of the dapper young men to poke fun at Benedick fall flat. Benedick no longer plays along. His serious aspect exposes the less pleasant side of the young noblemen, whose callous behaviour becomes glaringly apparent. In a scene that veers between the touching and the farcical, Leonato and Antonio, his brother, have just challenged Claudio and Don Pedro, vowing to seek revenge for the humiliation of Hero. Once they have left, Claudio scoffs at the impotence of the old men. He then demands of Benedick to fulfil his customary role of jester and amuse them: 'We have been up and down to seek thee, for we are high-proof melancholy and would fain have it beaten away. Wilt thou use thy wit?' (5.1.122–4). In the wake of the brutality of the church scene, the insensitivity of the young blades is striking. But Benedick refuses to be drawn into the badinage that they expect from him and delivers his challenge in deadly earnest, adding 'I jest not' (143). Claudio's stab at wit to taunt Benedick miscarries. 'I thank him, he hath bid me to a calf's head and a capon, the which if I do not carve most curiously, say my knife's naught. Shall I not find a woodcock too?', he sneers, attempting to cast a slur on Benedick's courage by insinuating that he resembles beasts associated with cowardice and stupidity, a calf, a capon, which was a castrated rooster, and a woodcock (151–4). Here Claudio tries to deploy humour in a game of one-upmanship with Benedick and to deride him for deviating from the codes they previously shared. But wit is not Claudio's strong point. As Benedick drily remarks, 'Sir, your wit ambles well; it goes easily' (155). By analogy with a horse, Claudio's wit moves at a leisurely pace, without the quickness and sting of a truly cutting quip. Without Benedick as a member of the trio, the stylish young men are bereft of a whetstone on which to sharpen their wits.

Repartee

When Beatrice and Benedick are on stage together, sparks fly – we get a rapid crossfire of quick, clever remarks and retorts. The tension between the two antagonists – both their fury and their fascination with each other – is palpable. Leonato has prepared us for their encounter with his comment, 'They never meet but there's a skirmish of wit between them' (1.1.59–60). If Beatrice labels Benedick as 'Signor Mountanto' (28), Benedick addresses her as 'Lady Disdain' (114), alluding to her pride and arrogance towards potential suitors. At the same time, he hastens to add that for his part he has nothing but scorn for women. Beatrice pounces on his remark, derisively applauding his abstention from women as good news for her sex. As she elaborates, 'I had rather hear my dog bark at a crow, than a man swear he loves me' (1.1.125). The duel of wits continues at a breathless pace:

BENEDICK

God keep your ladyship still in that mind, so some gentleman or other shall scape a predestinate scratched face.

BEATRICE

Scratching would not make it worse, an 'twere such a face as yours were.

BENEDICK

Well, you are a rare parrot-teacher.

BEATRICE

A bird of my tongue is better than a beast of yours.

BENEDICK

I would my horse had the speed of your tongue, and so good a continuer. But keep your way, o'God's name; I have done.

BEATRICE

You always end with a jade's trick; I know you of old.

(126–39)

Benedick promptly echoes her congratulations to womankind in general at his lack of interest in pursuing them – by greeting her own avowal of disinterest as a narrow escape for his own sex. Beatrice counters by disparaging his appearance. In return, Benedick makes a jibe about her garrulousness and lack of originality, comparing her to someone teaching a parrot to speak by endlessly repeating the same words. The tilting match descends into a barrage of metaphors of beasts and birds, both sides winding up by alleging that the other is reminiscent of a horse. Benedick claims that in her loquacity Beatrice resembles a horse of boundless energy who never tires, while Beatrice accuses him of being like vicious horse who throws off its rider and runs off, as Benedick is doing, sneaking away from the argument.

Some critics detect a reference to a possible previous affair in Beatrice's final remark about knowing Benedick's tricks from the past. The evidence they cite is a conversation between Don Pedro and Beatrice, in which the Prince gently admonishes her for her scathing treatment of his friend, declaring, 'you have lost the heart of Signor Benedick'. Beatrice defends herself with a cryptic explanation. 'Indeed, my lord, he lent it me awhile, and I gave him use for it, a double heart for his single one', she explains, and goes on to state, 'once before he won it of me with false dice' (2.1.253–7). Employing imagery from the practice of usury and games of chance, she admits that Benedick once gained her love – she returned the heart he lent her with an interest rate ('use') of 100 per cent. However, she then asserts that he won her heart by cheating in the game of love. It is certainly true that in his plays Shakespeare is apt to strew hints of a previous history in connection with his characters, adroitly creating the impression of real-life people. Generations of actors have put these suggestions into practice by inter-preting the relationship between the two opponents as one freighted with a narrative of betrayal, and their bandying of barbed jokes as a defence mechanism to protect themselves from pain.

To be sure, the couple's sardonic repartee continues even after they have admitted their love to each other. When Benedick requests Margaret to send a message to Beatrice, requesting her to come and see him, he is overcome by surprise that she actually complies. 'Sweet Beatrice, wouldst thou come when I called thee?', he asks in wonder. 'Yea signor, and depart when you bid me', is Beatrice's ironic riposte (5.2.41–2).

BENEDICK
O, stay but till then.
BEATRICE
'Then' is spoken; fare you well now.

(42–4)

Beatrice turns Benedick's words around in her customary caustic manner, wilfully misconstruing his words. She continues to poke fun at her lover's sugary tone throughout their exchange, leading him to abandon his attempt at playing the romantic wooer and to admit 'Thou and I are too wise to woo peaceably' (67). Neither he nor Beatrice are cut out for the conventional role of lover, mouthing sentimental platitudes. What unites them is their unconventional stance towards social bromides and their cleverness in turning commonplaces upside down. He rallies to regain his own keen wit, mock-lecturing her that in an age that sets a premium on stylish manners and outward show it is imperative to promote oneself shamelessly to rise in status. 'If a man do not erect in this age his own tomb ere he dies, he shall live no longer in monument than the bell rings and the widow weeps' – which, as he explains, is no longer than an hour in the case of mourning bells and a quarter of an hour in the case of a mourning widow. 'Therefore is it most expedient for the wise, if Don Worm – his conscience – find no impediment to the contrary, to be the trumpet of his own virtues' (71–9). In the cynical words of a social renegade who has turned his back on the path for advancement by deserting his patron, Don Pedro, and the club of courtiers gathered around him,

Shakespeare delivers a mordant comment on the culture of manners that spread throughout Europe in the wake of Castiglione's handbook for courtly aspirants. The metaphor of one's conscience as a worm derives from the Bible, but the stinging jab – 'Don Worm' – at the Prince he previously served, Don Pedro, is Benedick's invention.

On the very verge of marriage, Beatrice and Benedick shy away from the implications of entering into a state that might trammel their freedom and stifle their hunger for independence. Before taking the plunge, Benedick turns to Beatrice one last time to reassure himself that he is making the right decision. The dialogue that ensues is a brilliant piece of comic business that hilariously sends up romantic norms and offers a parody of the solemn reunion between Claudio and Hero that immediately precedes it, a scene that appears to whitewash the cruelty that wrecked the first wedding with a coat of syrupy sentimentality. The exchange between Benedick and Beatrice is radically different.

BENEDICK
    Do not you love me?
BEATRICE   Why no, no more than reason.
BENEDICK
    Why then your uncle and the prince and Claudio
    Have been deceived – they swore you did.
BEATRICE
    Do not you love me?
BENEDICK   Troth no, no more than reason.
BEATRICE
    Why then my cousin, Margaret and Ursula
    Are much deceived, for they swear you did.
BENEDICK
    They swore that you were almost sick for me.
BEATRICE
    They swore that you were well-nigh dead for me.
BENEDICK
    'Tis no such matter. Then you do not love me?

BEATRICE
No truly, but in friendly recompense.

(5.4.74–83)

In supple, synchronized lines, this time in verse, Beatrice and Benedick re-enact their badinage from earlier scenes, mockingly echoing each other's words almost verbatim in order to strenuously deny any notion of a deeper rapport between them. Beatrice and Benedick make it clear that they have no wish to follow in the footsteps of Claudio and Hero, rejecting the romantic fictions of marriage that hold sway in the society of Messina. It is only when their own sonnets are brandished under their noses that they are willing to set their scruples aside. Ironically, it takes one of the most formulaic of all romantic fictions, the sonnet, to overcome their innate reluctance to accept social conventions and enter into the bond of marriage.

Malapropism

What all members of Messina society share is a love of words. Some of them are particularly gifted in the use of language. Others are atrocious. The scenes with Dogberry and his men offer a spoof of a world infatuated with elaborate speech. The master constable and his cohorts are petty social aspirants who are anxious to ape their betters, but end up massacring the English language. The main device Shakespeare uses in the comic subplot of the play is *malapropism*, a term that denotes the use of an inappropriate word instead of one that sounds similar. The result is often very funny. The word malapropism itself originates from Richard Sheridan's play *The Rivals* (1775). Mrs Malaprop is a character who is at pains to sound genteel, but gets things badly wrong. In the nineteenth century the term 'Dogberryism' was coined as a label for the very same comic effect.

Like Beatrice and Benedick, the troop of watchmen is

Shakespeare's invention. There is no mention of a comic subplot in the sources for the play. Dogberry and the members of the watch appear fairly late in the play, in Act 3, after Don John has begun injecting venom into the ears of Claudio and the Prince with his contrived allegations against Hero, and has succeeded in poisoning the magical mood of the action. Unlike the characters of the main plot, the low-life characters are distinctly un-Italian. They are carbon copies of provincial English watchmen. Their very names demonstrate their rustic origins. Dogberry was the name of the fruit of a common plant, the dogwood; Verges was possibly derived from 'verjuice', the sour juice of unripe grapes or other fruit, which was used in cooking. The name might also refer to the verge, the staff of office carried by those in authority. The names of the other citizens, George Seacoal and Hugh Oatcake, have rural connotations (McEachern 2016: 186). The term 'clown', which today we associate with a comedian or a comic role in a play, originally referred to a country bumpkin (Wiles 1987). For an audience of Londoners, yokels from the countryside were an inexhaustible source of humour. The fact that many of the spectators had themselves only recently moved to the metropolis, or had urban credentials that barely reached back a generation, only served to reinforce their pleasure at laughing at outsiders who lacked urban sophistication.

A nationwide police force was only introduced in England in the nineteenth century. During the Elizabethan age, policing was organized locally, with a citizen patrol responsible to justices of the peace, traditionally appointed from members of the landowning classes. In *Much Ado About Nothing*, Leonato seems to fulfil the latter function. Dogberry and Verges approach him shortly before the wedding scene and request a word with him, announcing, 'Our watch, sir, have indeed comprehended two auspicious persons, and we would have them this morning examined before your worship' (3.5.43–5). They deliver such a confused version of their findings that Leonato has no idea what they are talking about. It is a moment of tantalizing suspense in the play, soaked in dramatic irony – the audience knows exactly what the clowns are labouring to convey and watch in dismay as their message miscarries. Leonato remains blissfully unaware of the fact that what he is receiving is a warning about the catastrophe that is about to ensue in the following scene and blight the life of his daughter and himself. Apart from ratcheting up the tension, the scene is also hilarious. Within one single sentence Dogberry manages to mangle two crucial words: what he presumably wants to say is that they have 'apprehended' (or arrested) two 'suspicious' persons, making a grandiloquent attempt to express himself in a formal, legalistic register quite beyond his grasp. In actual fact, Dogberry and his companion have 'comprehended' nothing at all. The characters of the main plot, however, will later understand their fatal error. The information the watch have uncovered is of vital importance and is the key to exposing the egregious lies that Don John and his henchmen have planted. In this sense, their discovery is highly 'auspicious', promising a fortunate outcome to the plot and instrumental in averting the tragedy towards which the narrative appears to be plunging. In a grotesque twist, the linguistic mistakes of the clowns contain the kernel of a deeper truth.

It is the method which inheres in the verbal madness of the low-life characters that makes their blunders so ingenious and amusing. Sometimes they simply get muddled by big words. When Dogberry demands of his acolytes whether they be 'good men and true', his deputy Verges throws in, 'Yea, or else it were pity but they should suffer salvation, body and soul' (3.3.2–3). The humour derives from the fact that salvation, the yearned-for end of every human being in the Christian faith, is hardly a destiny one 'suffers' – quite the contrary. Probably Verges means to say 'damnation', the exact opposite of 'salvation'. Similarly, when Dogberry pontificates that 'for the watch to babble and to talk is most tolerable' (35–6) – he means 'intolerable' – the result is absurd. In effect, what his words do is draw attention to his own imbecility, babbling endless nonsense while lording it over others. Dogberry and his

companions (to the extent they get a word in edgeways) are so
keen to strut their command of high-flown language that they
get things plain wrong. Dogberry wishes to have the Sexton
set down their 'excommunication' (meaning 'examination')
(3.5.59); Verges declares that they have the 'exhibition' to
examine (meaning 'commission') (4.2.5). Dogberry assures
Leonato that their examination of the prisoners will be 'suffi-
gance' (for 'sufficient') (3.5.48) and admonishes his men to
be 'vigitant' (for 'vigilant') (3.3.91). Emulating his superior,
deputy constable Seacoal demands of the villains, 'Let us obey
you to go with us' (3.3.168) – intending to say the opposite.
And Dogberry absurdly reproves the knaves for being 'full of
piety' (4.2.80). He is also fond of showing off his knowledge,
and liberally sprinkles his speech with proverbs. Unfortunately,
they are quite irrelevant in the context in which he uses them.
He advises the men of the watch to avoid any contact with
criminals, lecturing them that 'they that touch pitch will
be defiled', citing a well-known biblical saying (3.3.55–6).
The joke lies his complete ignorance of the meaning of the
expression, which is a warning to avoid the company of the
rich and the temptations it entails, not to avoid arresting
felons, which is, after all, the task of the watch. Dogberry
is also quite deaf to irony. In the presence of Leonato, he is
anxious to belittle his companion, Verges, as a garrulous old
duffer. Leonato ironically remarks, 'he comes too short of
you', which Dogberry smugly pockets as a compliment: 'Gifts
that God gives' (3.5.40–1).

Sometimes, however, the members of the watch and above
all their self-inflated leader get words wrong in a way that
is perversely right. 'This is your charge', Dogberry intones
sonorously, 'you shall comprehend all vagrom men' (3.3.24–5).
The word 'vagrom' is a nonsensical coinage that seems to
meld the terms 'vagrant' with 'roam', which neatly sums up
what homeless people, large groups of whom swarmed the
country in the 1590s in search of employment, did. When
Dogberry praises his deputy as 'desertless' and 'senseless'
(3.3.9; 22) we have no doubt that he (inadvertently) is spot

on. Nor would we quarrel with the gist of his description of Verges, the headborough, whom he is fond of cutting down to size as someone whose 'wits are not so blunt' as he would desire them (3.5.10) – what he means to say is something quite different. In the dross that Dogberry produces, there is often a hidden nugget of truth. He obsequiously thanks Leonato for the generous reward he bestows on him, calling him 'a most thankful and reverent youth' and urging him to 'correct himself' (5.1.304–5; 311). As spectators of Leonato's harsh outburst against his own daughter at the wedding, we couldn't agree with him more. In the burlesque interrogation scene, Dogberry rounds on Borachio in fury at his having described Don John as a villain from whom he had extracted a thousand ducats for maligning Hero. An inveterate toady to all members of the ruling class, he brands the accomplices of Don John as criminals guilty of 'perjury' and 'burglary' (4.2.44; 52). Curiously, he is right, but not in the sense that he means these accusations. Don John and his clique are undoubtedly guilty of lying, and their slanderous actions rob Hero of every shred of dignity. And Dogberry's insistence to the Sexton that the orotund term 'malefactors' must refer to himself and his partner (4.2.3–4) hits the nail on its head. The constables break innumerable laws of correct speech.

Dogberry and Company serve to lighten the mood of the play, particularly in the second half. But the clowns also fulfil a further purpose. As so often in Shakespeare's subplots, the low-life characters offer a parody of the action of the main plot. Like the noble members of Messina society, the constable and the watch misunderstand every word they hear, and misread what is taking place under their very eyes. Miraculously delivered a confession by the perpetrators of the plot against Hero on a silver platter, they are too obtuse to grasp the truth. Instead, they remain in thrall to their misconceptions about the superior nature of the higher-born, too busy being deferential to the aristocracy to realize the import of what they are hearing. In addition to the sordid commercial details about Don John's conspiracy, one of the watchmen

reports that during the conversation they have overheard
Borachio announce exactly what will happen on the day of
the wedding, revealing the information that Claudio intends
to denounce Hero in front of the whole assembly and
break off the nuptials. Dogberry's response is to explode in
anger against Borachio. 'O villain! Thou wilt be condemned
into everlasting redemption for this', he expostulates with
the suspect (4.2.55–9). Characteristically, he stumbles over
his words, substituting 'redemption' for 'damnation'. What
creates the irony is the fact that Borachio was faithfully
conveying the truth of the matter. The atrocious behaviour
during the wedding is Claudio's, not Borachio's. Slyly, the play
comments on the actions of the noble characters by having the
servile and doltish constables articulate sentiments that they
would never dream of saying were their remarks not directed
at the wrong addressee. Paradoxically, the term Dogberry
mistakenly uses, 'redemption', is precisely what Borachio's
confession enables the characters of the main plot to gain,
and what prevents the narrative from hurtling inexorably into
tragedy. Once again, Dogberry accurately recapitulates the
events of the story – without ever grasping the plot.

The elite of Messina misapprehend what they perceive
for different reasons, of course. They are swayed by other
ideological considerations – not deference to the higher tiers of
society, but the staunch belief that women are innately corrupt
and, given the slightest opportunity, prone to betray men.
But Dogberry combines a forelock-tugging stance towards
his betters with an overweening arrogance towards those he
deems inferior to him on the social scale. Patronizing towards
his companions, his overbearing manner towards the men
under arrest bears more than a hint of threat. The swagger
of a minor official is miles away from the suave behaviour
of the members of high society, but the self-importance he
exudes might well remind us of more powerful characters in
the play who never question their right to manipulate others
and destroy lives at will. The callous cross-examination of
Hero during her aborted wedding is immediately replayed

in a comic key in the interrogation of Borachio and Conrade by Dogberry in the following scene. For all their differences, the Prince and his coterie and Dogberry and his men conduct themselves in strikingly similar fashion, blatantly misreading signs and attempting to browbeat those they consider guilty of transgressions.

The Prince, Claudio and Leonato are only too susceptible to the performance at Hero's window staged for their consumption, since it tallies with the preconceptions they harbour. They see what they expect to see. But they are also gullible to illusions because they live in a world where superficialities and appearances are what counts. In their hunger for social recognition, Dogberry and his companions provide a caricature of the culture of elegant manners with which their betters are preoccupied. Their fascination with status and their farcical failure to acquire the thin coat of polish they crave makes for some of the most ludicrous moments in the play. It is their distorted use of language that lays bare their woeful inadequacy in the discipline of style and grace.

The linguistic confusion of the clowns reflects their view of social priorities – one that resembles the attitudes of the more sophisticated characters to a remarkable degree. Dogberry lauds one of his men, George Seacoal, for his outward aspect, and proclaims 'To be a well-favoured man is the gift of fortune, but to write and read comes by nature' (3.3.14–15). No doubt Dogberry intends to pronounce a sententious statement about the importance of learning, but what he actually delivers is a vindication of surface appearances as superior to acquired skills. He goes on to dismiss Seacoal's education – 'for your writing and reading, let that appear when there is no need of such vanity' – before appointing him as the leading officer of the watch (20–1). To hear learning described as 'vanity' is of course a joke, but Dogberry only articulates what exponents of the culture of style put more elegantly when they belittle the need for true erudition in favour of a smattering of learning, useful chiefly in making polite conversation. Dogberry's exhortations to his crew uncannily echoes precepts presented in manuals of courtesy. It is of paramount importance, he urges, to avoid giving offence to any man (78–9). Advice framed for social occasions is lampooned by being voiced in the context of crime prevention, where one might suppose the opposite to hold true. Indeed, Dogberry's men conclude that their best course of action would lie in sleeping on their watch (37–41).

When the men are on their beat and overhear Borachio's conversation with Conrade in which he reveals details of the plot to destroy Hero's alliance, they are too oafish to grasp the significance of what they are hearing. Instead, they jumble up odds and ends of dialogue and misinterpret them in the light of their own preoccupation with social rank. Borachio holds a brief disquisition on fashion and airily uses a figure of speech to illustrate his point, personifying fashion as a 'deformed thief' in order to allude to the distorting effects of outward show. In a comical aside, a dim-witted watchman reveals that he takes the metaphor literally. 'I know that Deformed. 'A has been a vile thief this seven year; 'a goes up and down like a gentleman; I remember his name', he announces portentously (120–3). Needless to say, he remembers no such thing, since there is no person of that name. Later, one of his colleagues exclaims, 'I know him, 'a wears a lock' (162–3). The thief, Deformed, allegedly apes the gentry both in apparel and in his fashionable accessories, such as a long lock of hair known as a love-lock. When Dogberry passes on this invaluable piece of information to his superior, Leonato, he embellishes it further: 'they say he wears a key in his ear and a lock hanging by it, and borrows money in God's name, the which he hath used so long and never paid that now men grow hard-hearted and will lend nothing for God's sake' (5.1.298–302). Dogberry adds to the muddle by mixing up the lock of hair with a lock and key, which the phantom thief supposedly wears as an earring. What emerges is a variant of Chinese whispers about a non-existent person. This is a send-up of the similar set-up in Act 1 Scenes 2 and 3, when we observe gossip and hearsay in action, and the news of Don Pedro's intention to woo Hero in the name of Claudio mutates into a different story altogether.

Significantly, the chief offence of the imaginary crook seems to consist of his masquerading as a member of a class to which he does not by rights belong. In other words, he shares affinities with Dogberry and his band of social hopefuls. In his zeal to condemn the social imposter, the constable bungles the details of his denunciation. As members of the audience would know only too well, far from a sign of base origins, being in debt was a typically aristocratic gesture demonstrating one's nonchalance about trivial commercial concerns. By castigating the financial irresponsibility of the fictive charlatan, the clown only exposes his own ignorance of fashionable behaviour.

For Dogberry, the crime of Conrade far outweighs the near-fatal slander to which Hero was subjected by Borachio. Dogberry is outraged that Conrade should label him as an ass. Needless to say, with every word he utters in his defence he proves Conrade right.

> I am a wise fellow, and which is more, an officer, and which is more, a householder, and which is more, as pretty a piece of flesh as any is in Messina, and one that knows the law – go to! – and a rich fellow enough – go to! – and a fellow that hath losses, and one that hath two gowns, and everything handsome about him.
>
> (4.2.81–7)

Indignantly, Dogberry enumerates his stellar qualities. He brags of his position, his standing, his pleasing exterior, his education and his affluence. Acquiring prestige is the main motivation in life for this petty official, as it is for his betters in Messina high society. His grotesque abuse of language serves to satirize the social pretensions that impel his actions. Ingratiating to his superiors, he is consumed by the desire to assert his place to those he considers beneath him in the social hierarchy. Nothing poses a greater threat to his sense of self-importance than to have a person he deems of lower rank defy his authority. He implores Leonato to mete out stringent punishment to the culprits. One suspects that in his eyes, the true atrocity is the defamation of his character. Status is the pre-eminent principle in his universe. During the interrogation of the prisoners, Dogberry insists that the deposition be taken with due respect paid to rank order. 'Write down, that they hope they serve God; and write God first, for God defend but God should go before such villains' (4.2.20–1), he commands. In Dogberry's worldview, even God sets store by correct precedence.

Clowns and fools

The quarto edition of *Much Ado About Nothing*, which appeared in 1600, is the only version of the play to survive from Shakespeare's lifetime. What it reveals is the fingerprints of the playwright and his company at work. One instance is the presence of 'ghost' characters such as Innogen, the wife of Leonato, who is listed as entering the stage at the beginning of Acts 1 and 2 but never says a word. She seems to be the vestige of an original design which was never carried out – to include a mother for Hero in the cast of characters. As the play stands, it is far more persuasive to have Hero as the motherless daughter of a patriarchal father whose only female guidance is that of her cousin, Beatrice. Critics have commented on the dearth of mothers in Shakespeare's plays (Adelman 1992). Daughters growing up without mothers are legion and populate plays from the *The Taming of the Shrew* to *King Lear*. In point of fact, the reasons might well lie in practical as well as artistic reasons. On the early modern stage, female characters were played by boy actors. Talented as they seem to have been, playing a mature woman was particularly demanding, and Shakespeare and his company might have required the best players for the other important female roles in the play.

'Innogen' survives into the First Folio, the first collected edition of Shakespeare's works. Another trace of the earlier edition that is to be found in the First Folio is a discrepancy in the speech prefixes in Act 4 Scene 2. The lines of Dogberry and Verges sometimes appear under the names of the performers who played these roles, William Kemp and Richard Cowley. Kemp was one the leading comedians of Shakespeare's company while it was still called the Lord Chamberlain's Men and frequently played comic duos together with Cowley as a straight man. As one of the leading chroniclers of Shakespeare's theatrical career, Bart van Es, notes, the role of Dogberry was almost certainly written specifically with Kemp in mind. Kemp must have attained star status during his time with the Chamberlain's Men. One of his main lines in humour was stumbling over big words, a technique that he had already demonstrated to hilarious effect in earlier roles such as Bottom in *A Midsummer Night's Dream* (1595). Many of the other famous clown parts in Shakespeare's comedies are associated with him: Lance in *The Two Gentlement of Verona* (1590–1), Costard in *Love's Labour's Lost* (1594–5), Peter in *Romeo and Juliet* (1595) and Lancelot in *The Merchant of Venice* (1596–7). Some scholars such as David Wiles believe that the figure of Falstaff was created for him, too. Kemp's comic persona was usually that of a plain, blunt man armed with a quantum of cunning. The roles often involve direct address to the audience and provide considerable leeway for improvisation. Kemp was also famous as a producer of jigs, musical routines that were regularly performed at the end of plays (tragedies as well as comedies). Jigs were known for their boisterous, bawdy humour and ballad elements, and were an ideal vehicle to showcase Kemp's physical dexterity.

When the Lord Chamberlain's Men relocated to Southwark in 1599, dismantling and then reassembling their previous theatre building, The Theatre, on the new site and calling it the Globe Theatre, Kemp was still part of the company. In fact, he was one of the five players who were involved in the financial venture of the Globe, contributing to its costs in return for a share of the profits. However, for unknown reasons, Kemp left the Lord Chamberlain's Men, probably in 1600, and set out to forge a further career for himself as a solo performer. His most famous stunt was to dance all the way from London to Norwich, a feat that took a month and earned him a considerable amount of money as a return on sums speculated on his accomplishing the deed. He described the trip in a pamphlet with the title *Kemps Nine Daies Wonder* (1600).

The contrast to the new comedian who took his place at the Globe, both as sharer and chief comic, is striking. Robert Armin was known for his wit, his singing and his line in philosophical clowning. Unlike Kemp, he was not given to improvisation. It is probable that Shakespeare invented the figure of the wise fool specifically to fit his talents. Characters such as Touchstone in *As You Like It* (1599–1600), Feste in *Twelfth Night* (1600–1) and the Fool in *King Lear* (1605–6) are the most articulate figures on stage and show no linguistic clumsiness. Armin prided himself on his strain of intellectual humour, as displayed in his works *Quips upon Questions* and *Fool upon Fool* (both 1600). He built his persona around the real-life figure of the court jester, but gave it an indelible stamp of its own. Shakespeare's humour can be seen as emerging from a profound exploration of modes of comedy in collaboration with a small select band of his fellow actors. As van Es points out, Armin

> was a fellow creative thinker who introduced ways of thinking about comedy quite different from any that had earlier been evident in Shakespeare's plays. Cruelty, insanity, and absurdist poetry would – with increasing complexity – become an element in the drama that Shakespeare produced.
>
> (2013: 179)

In the course of Shakespeare's artistic trajectory his comic use of language underwent a drastic change. Dogberry's strain of humour, consisting predominantly of garbled speech, would be replaced by a subtle play with ambiguity and double meanings in which language would be used as a razor-sharp tool to profoundly question all authority. What would also change is the political valency of humour. The wise fools of the later plays are outsider figures, licensed fools who are permitted to voice doubts that would not be acceptable in other characters. As Viola puts it in *Twelfth Night*, 'There is no slander in an allowed fool' (1.5.90). Above all, they are individualists who are uninterested in forging close bonds with other human beings. By contrast, Dogberry and his cohorts are upholders of the social order, anxious to please their betters and 'offend no man' (3.3.79). There is, however, a touch of something unpleasant about these inconsequential figures of local authority. While addressing Leonato, Dogberry takes care to snub the headborough, Verges, reminding him of his place: 'An two men ride of a horse, one must ride behind' (3.5.35–6). The arrest of the villains of the piece, Borachio and Conrad, is on purely arbitrary grounds, and during the cross-examination Dogberry menacingly informs Borachio 'I do not like thy face' (4.2.46). The thread of submerged violence running throughout the play is also reflected in Dogberry's veiled threats.

Current performances attempt to compensate for the fact that the verbal humour of the play is difficult for a modern audience to follow by inserting additional comic business. In Joss Whedon's 2012 film version, Dogberry and Verges are security guards of singular obtuseness who succeed in locking themselves out of their own car. In Kenneth Branagh's 1993 version, Dogberry, played by Michael Keaton, seems a strangely demented figure who goes around pretending he is riding a horse. He exudes a sense of aggression barely held in check and all his subordinates are terrified of him. It is also apparent that the prisoners have been severely maltreated. Both film versions convey a sinister air about the clowns that has a firm basis in the characters Shakespeare portrays.

Writing matters

1   In this chapter we have sketched the historical context in which the play is set. This is helpful in grasping many of the allusions that might be lost to us today, but it is certainly possible to adapt the play to an entirely different background. If you were to direct a production of the play, where would you set it? Do some of the aspects discussed in connection with the Renaissance culture of manners hold true for other cultural contexts? Try to put together a blueprint of a production of the play that would address these elements in a completely different setting.

2   Look for other examples of a convoluted, euphuistic style in the play. When does it seem to work well and when does it seem to be overly mannered? It might be helpful to bear in mind that nonchalance is the main effect that users of stylish speech would be aiming for.

3   Look for more examples of wit by either Beatrice or Benedick and analyse them carefully. Do you detect further differences in their styles of wit?

4   Choose one scene – for instance, the masque in Act 2 Scene 1 – and analyse the dialogue carefully in terms of wit.

5   Analyse all the examples of malapropism that you can find in the play. When does the misuse of language ironically bear other meanings?

6   Look at the setting of Italy in a number of plays. In what way does the setting shape the themes of the play significantly? The play closely aligned with *Much Ado About Nothing*, *Love's Labour's Lost*, is set in France, not Italy. Does the setting nevertheless share elements in common with that of *Much Ado About Nothing*?

7   Look at the wit of Falstaff in *Henry IV Parts 1* and *2*.

How does his style of language resemble that of Beatrice and Benedick, and how does it differ?

8   Compare the scenes of repartee between Benedick and Beatrice with similar scenes in other plays, for instance *Love's Labour's Lost*. Are there differences as well as similarities?

9   Look at the dialogue between Cesario (Viola) and Olivia in *Twelfth Night*. Does wit play a role? If so, try to find examples. Who is the wittiest character in the play?

10 Look closely at the jokes about cuckoldry. When do they seem to you to be gibes aimed at women and when do they seem to be above all about male bonding? Or are things more complex? Take a look at how Iago plays with Othello's anxieties about being cuckolded. Is there, for example, a difference between Benedick and Iago in the way they use the imagery of cuckoldry?

11 Look at the imagery of cuckoldry in *The Winter's Tale*. What happens to the imagery of betrayal in the later play? Look carefully at the language, particularly the speeches by Leontes.

12 Compare the flirtation between Beatrice and Benedick with that between Ganymede (or Rosalind) and Orlando in *As You Like It*. There, too, Ganymede makes allusions to cuckoldry. Analyse the similarities in the relationships between the lovers in both plays.

13 Look at the tension between same-sex friendship and marriage in plays like *The Two Gentlemen of Verona*, *The Merchant of Venice* or *Romeo and Juliet*. Do they treat the theme in a similar manner to *Much Ado About Nothing*, or are there differences?

14 Compare Dogberry with other comic figures in Shakespeare's plays, for example Lance and Speech in *The Two Gentlemen of Verona*, the Dromios in *The*

Comedy of Errors, Costard in *Love's Labour's Lost*,
Bottom in *A Midsummer Night's Dream*, Lancelot in
The Merchant of Venice, Falstaff in *The Merry Wives
of Windsor* and so on. Analyse their language in terms
of strategies of creating humour.

15 Alternatively, look carefully at Dogberry's language
in comparison with the language of a wise fool
– Touchstone, Feste, or the Fool in *King Lear*.
Shakespeare uses linguistic abuse as a comic device in
other plays, too. What similarities do you detect, and
what differences?

CHAPTER TWO

Language:
Forms and uses

Rhetoric

If the characters of *Much Ado About Nothing* are all, in diverse ways, enthralled by language, this was a fascination that the entire nation shared. In the era of Shakespeare, English was still in the process of becoming a language of nuance and sophistication, one that was a source of national identity and pride. The Renaissance was an age of discovery and expanding horizons, and even England, long ravaged by civil wars and dynastic infighting, caught the spirit of the times. The invention of the printing press, the birth of an increasingly international market economy and an upsurge in trade opened the nation to an influx of foreign influences. New words poured into the country, leaving their trace on the spoken language as well as the literary culture. English was by no means the stable language it would become in the course of the eighteenth century, and at this point in time it was endlessly malleable, both in usage and in orthography. Shakespeare alone has been attributed with creating several thousand new words, although his linguistic inventiveness may have been overrated. What made his language and that of his peers so remarkable is perhaps less their coinage of new words and phrases than the flexibility with which they put words together in original ways, which made their language rich and startling. Audiences of the time were particularly receptive to the power of the spoken word, and the Reformation spawned a host of charismatic preachers whose fiery sermons regularly drew huge congregations. Curiously, the pulpit and the stage were keen competitors in a burgeoning culture of entertainment, in which the same audiences moved from sermon to play and back again. Spectacle certainly played no mean part in attracting large crowds, both in the form of popular entertainments such as bear-baiting and executions and in spectacular scenes recreated on stage, but the allure of resonant language was a decisive factor in appealing to the early modern public.

At the beginning of the sixteenth century, men of letters such as Sir Thomas More would turn to Latin to create their literary masterpieces. *Utopia* was published in 1516 in Latin and not until 1551, many years after More had been executed, did it appear in an English translation by Ralph Robinson. More's friend Erasmus wrote his own works in Latin too, including his satirical essay, *In Praise of Folly*, first printed in 1511, which was dedicated to More. Its original title, *Moriae Encomium*, was a clever pun on More's name: the phrase could also be taken to mean 'in praise of More'. Latin was not only the language of church liturgy and ecclesiastical administration, but the official medium of court diplomacy and jurisprudence throughout the Western world. It was the language of the *literati* all over Europe, who were certain of gaining a wide readership for their work if they wrote in this *lingua franca* of the educated strata of society. It is true that great writing was produced in Middle English by writers based at court, notably Geoffrey Chaucer, thought to be the Father of English literature. But during the early modern age, the idea that the vernacular might serve as a medium for literature was mainly inspired by developments in Italy. Dante was one of the first to advocate writing in Italian; even though Petrarch demurred, considering the vernacular to be the language of the uneducated masses and producing his most ambitious work in Latin, his sonnets or *Canzoniere*, written in Italian, sparked a revolution in poetry that swept over Europe. Together with Dante and Boccaccio, Petrarch served as a model for Italian style; his development of the sonnet form was imported into numerous other European languages, including English. The genre was adopted so successfully that a specific 'English' form of sonnet emerged, adapted to the strengths and weaknesses of the English language – for instance, the relative paucity of rhyming words as compared to Italian. Shakespeare was not the only poet to utilize the form, but his iconic status has led later generations to call it the 'Shakespearean' sonnet. The early modern period emerged as a golden age of literature in English, producing a vibrant culture of prose, poetry and drama by writers such as Sir Thomas Wyatt, Sir Philip Sidney, Edmund Spenser, Christopher Marlowe, Ben Jonson and other contemporaries of Shakespeare, whose work jostled each other at court, in print and on stage. A spirit of nationalism took hold of the English and was an added incentive to produce works in English that could rival those of other cultural nations, in particular Italy, the cradle of the Renaissance.

The intellectual movement that dominated Renaissance Europe, Humanism, played a complex yet decisive role in promoting the vernacular as a literary language. Chiefly concerned with re-establishing the works of classical antiquity to pride of place in early modern culture, Humanists were appalled at the excrescences and corrupt practices that had accrued in translations from Latin during the Middle Ages. They launched a campaign to purge the language and encourage its correct usage, above all in educational institutions. At the same time, Humanist scholars immersed themselves in philological studies of canonical medieval texts. The most canonical text was the Vulgate, the Latin Bible that had been in use since the fourth century. By returning to the Greek original, Erasmus discovered numerous errors in the Latin translation, and brought out his own bilingual Greek and Latin edition of the New Testament in 1516. Although the aim of scholars like Erasmus was to recover the Holy Word and restore its pristine meaning, the effect was to undermine the authority of the Roman Catholic Church, which viewed any deviation from the official Vulgate with suspicion. Erasmus's edition spurred a wave of Bible translations into the vernacular, often by Reformers, amongst them the German Bible published by Martin Luther in 1522, the New Testament translation published by William Tyndale in 1526 and Jacques Lefèvre d'Étaples' French translation in 1530.

With its emphasis on learning, Humanism was instrumental in instigating what has been termed 'the educational revolution' (Stone 1964) in the entire continent. The pillar on which their concept of education was founded was the recovery of classical rhetoric. A crop of grammar schools sprang up all over England and generations of schoolboys wrestled their way through a rigorous regimen of the classics, studying Latin grammar and style in exhaustive detail. Rhetoric had been overshadowed by a focus on logic (or dialectic) in the medieval curriculum, tailored mainly to young scholars who would pursue a career in theology. Both dialectic and rhetoric involved learning the art of discourse and reasoned argumentation, but the difference lay in how the acquired skills were to be implemented. Dialectic was indispensable for the practice of scholasticism, a method of learning that accorded priority to a quest for truth through stringent reasoning. Humanists mocked scholastic thinkers, whom they dubbed the 'schoolmen', as pedants whose arid thought was grounded on hair-splitting and dogmatism. Instead, they rekindled an interest in rhetoric, which might be defined as the art of persuasion. The rediscovery of key texts by Aristotle, Cicero and Quintilian played a crucial role. The defence of rhetoric was based on the argument that eloquence and wisdom were inextricably bound up with each other: speaking well and thinking well were closely interlinked. It was not possible to gain wisdom without a mastery of eloquence, and vice versa. Rhetoric, these thinkers maintained, was not merely a technical craft, but was related to the domain of ethics. As

Cicero argued, it required the study of philosophy and the arts. According to Cicero, good speech and good action were intertwined; for Quintilian, a good orator was necessarily a man of wisdom. Since for humanists education was a means to train the ruling classes in virtue, the study of rhetoric was regarded as indispensable for good governance (Skinner 1978). In addition, humanists claimed that rhetoric was a civilizing tool, and was necessary to sway others towards virtue. In the foundational myth of rhetoric, civilization itself was first created by an orator. This myth, outlined by Cicero and recycled by Quintilian, was often repeated in the innumerable handbooks of rhetoric that appeared during the Renaissance, and was sometimes conflated with the biblical story of the Fall from Paradise and the Redemption (McAlindon 1973). In his *Rhetoric*, Aristotle spelt out the reasons why rhetoric was useful: it could help justice prevail in society and persuade people to the good, it was a means of self-defence, and it facilitated the discovery of the truth (Vickers 1988).

The method put forward to this end was a form of enquiry that required looking at diverse angles of an issue, or debating a question from both sides: *in utramque partem*, as the Latin phrase went. Doing so would create an awareness of the complexity of the problem and hence enable one to approximate the right answer to the extent possible. For Cicero, who largely endorsed the philosophical school of Academic Scepticism, it was impossible to gain access to full knowledge, but by rigorous reasoning it was certainly possible to approach the truth and to take action accordingly. This concept chimed perfectly with Cicero's training as an orator and a lawyer. Examining a case from different perspectives and deliberating on the most reasonable course to pursue were central to civil society in the Roman Republic. During his legal and political career, Cicero honed his skills in persuading his audience to share the viewpoint he was presenting, deploying the large arsenal of rhetorical devices that he set out in his writings. These did not merely involve strategies of argumentation (*logos*), but included an appeal to emotions (*pathos*) and making a convincing case for the credibility of the speaker (*ethos*). For Cicero, rhetoric was the foundation of political life. But by the time Quintilian wrote his authoritative manual of rhetoric, the *Institutio Oratoria*, the Republic had collapsed. Although eloquence remained a highly desirable accomplishment and continued to occupy an important position in education and jurisprudence, in the Middle Ages rhetoric in legislative assemblies and at court dwindled in importance, and the discipline was treated mainly as a formalized set of rules.

In early modern England, Humanist Reformers encouraged a revival of the study of rhetoric. Preaching the Word was regarded as a crucial instrument of the Reformation, and in religious instruction great weight was attached to the art of persuasive speech. Writing was also valued for its ability to win people to lead a virtuous life through an appeal to the reader's emotions. The generation of poets and playwrights who profited from the innovations in education in early modern England were steeped in the literature of antiquity and were meticulously groomed in rhetoric. As literary critics have long pointed out, the principle of approaching a topic from various angles was deeply influential in moulding English literature of this period. Literary writing staged debates in which the pros and cons of issues were carefully examined and compelling arguments on either side of a question were laid out. Style and structure became of paramount importance. Erasmus's rhetoric manual *De Copia* (1512), a guide to how to embellish one's speech and writing by means of variety and abundance of expression, became a school classic. Drama was particularly amenable to the influence of rhetorical modes of thought. As a genre, it embodied viewpoints rather than using a narrative voice to articulate them, as was largely the case in prose or in poetry. Admittedly, the literary genre of the dialogue could look back on a long, prestigious tradition in classical antiquity, and many of the texts studied in classrooms were written in this form. Recently critics such as Lynn Enterline have demonstrated how closely rhetorical teaching at school and at university was interwoven with practical exercises in writing and performing drama. Boys impersonated historical or mythical figures, or composed dialogues and acted them out. Academic drama was strongly endorsed as a means to practise the rhetorical skills of memorization and delivery. A favourite writing task known as *ethopoeia* involved devising speeches or letters by fictive characters drawn from classical mythology. It trained students to slip into the minds of a gamut of characters with whom they might have nothing in common and imaginatively recreate the world from their perspective. Shakespeare's gift for exploring the entire range of human characters and portraying their often conflicted inner lives without passing judgement on them – a gift that the poet Keats termed 'negative capability' – might be partly rooted in the rhetorical exercises he and his peers were set.

Rhetorical strategies in *Much Ado About Nothing*

In *Much Ado About Nothing*, the Renaissance concern with rhetoric has left its trace on several levels. The play is pervaded with an interest in verbal style and flaunts its versatility in linguistic expression. Wit, repartee, quips, elegant phrasing, eloquent set pieces and grotesque distortion of stylish speech all belong to its repertoire, as we have seen in Chapter 1. Clever symmetries in structure also reveal the fingerprints of Shakespeare's training in rhetoric. The two gulling scenes, in which Benedick and Beatrice are fooled by their friends into believing that the other is in love with them, are set side by side, in Act 2 Scene 3 and Act 3 Scene 1 respectively. This creates a mirror effect, which serves to reinforce the humour (doubling is often a potent comic device, as the theorist of humour Henri Bergson once pointed out), but it also allows us to compare the two scenes in terms of their similarities and differences. The misunderstandings of the low-life characters echo the misprision of the window show by the Prince and his cohorts; their battering of the English language is an inverse reflection of the sophisticated discourse of their betters. The moment in which Don Pedro unfolds his plan to trick the lovers (in Act 2 Scene 1) is immediately followed by a scene in which Don John discusses a plan to trick Claudio and his brother (Act 2 Scene 2), raising awkward questions about the parallels between the two plots. The inquisition of Hero at church is juxtaposed with a scene in which the vainglorious constable interrogates the crooks the watch have arrested. And so forth. Shakespeare's plays are cross-hatched with verbal echoes and submerged patterns, all of which contribute to their rich tapestry of meaning.

Disputing questions from divergent angles was a strategy ingrained in early modern culture. Writers were remarkably flexible in taking up a polemical stance, first in support of a position and then in opposition to it. A case in point is the debate about the role of women known as the *querelle des femmes*, or the battle of the sexes. It began in the late fourteenth century and raged all over Europe. Literary historians have become increasingly wary of drawing conclusions about the authors from their works denigrating or, conversely, in praise of women. Often the same writers would come down on either side of the issue. A highly influential masterpiece of Renaissance literature is the collection of tales by Boccaccio, *The Decameron*. The women he portrays are usually lascivious, scheming and seductive, although there are notable exceptions, such as the saintly Griselda, passive to the point of masochism, to use an anachronistic term. The female storytellers of the text, on the other hand, are refined and intelligent. Some years later, in 1374, Boccaccio produced a collection of lives of famous women, *De Mulieribus Claris*, which inspired numerous writers whose works were devoted to extolling the virtues of women, from Chaucer's *Legend of Good Women* in the 1380s, to Christine de Pizan's *Book of the City of Ladies* in 1405, to Sir Thomas Elyot's *Defence of Good Women* in 1540. But Boccaccio also wrote a darkly satirical work, *Il Corbaccio*, in which a first-person narrator is warned about the treachery of women. In Castiglione's *Book of the Courtier*, Book III is a replica of the *querelle des femmes*, with the interlocutors of the dialogue, a form that was not restricted to interaction between two speakers only, putting forward arguments both attacking women and in their defence. As critics have noted, the debate might not have been primarily about the role of women, but might have concealed a coded allusion to the emasculated position of courtiers in princely states. Amongst other things, the *querelle des femmes* was an exercise in style that offered writers an opportunity to display their intellectual acuity and literary artistry.

In *Much Ado About Nothing*, Benedick offers a comic example of the debate in a nutshell, condensed to a dispute within the same speaker. When we first see him, he is proud of his reputation as an enemy of women, 'a professed tyrant to their sex' (1.1.160–1). He is consternated that his companion, Claudio, has fallen in love and is contemplating marriage. Marriage in his eyes is automatically equated with female betrayal, and he lets loose a string of wisecracks about cuckoldry. His friends challenge him and vow to force him to change his tune, zestfully proceeding to cook up a plan to trip him up. When we see Benedick alone in the orchard at the beginning of the gulling scene, he is musing about the change Claudio has undergone. From once sharing his contempt for those in love, Claudio has now turned into a conventional lover, given over to effeminate pleasures and desires. In his soliloquy, Benedick wonders whether he too will succumb to the disease of love. 'May I be so converted and see with these eyes? I cannot tell; I think not'. He goes on to vow to do every-thing in his power to resist being made a fool of by a woman, using a characteristically funny and graphic image for a dupe of love. 'I will not be sworn but love may transform me to an oyster, but I'll take my oath on it, till he have made an oyster of me he shall never make me such a fool' (2.3.21–5). Even more amusing is the fact that although he has just sworn to abstain from yielding to love he begins to fantasize about the ideal woman, clinching the matter with a punning chiasmus, 'till all graces be in one woman, one woman shall not come in my grace' (27–8).

At the end of the very same scene, Benedick is forced to recant. He falls hook, line, and sinker for the fabricated story that Beatrice is in love with him and immediately decides, 'Why, it must be requited' (216). Ruefully, he reminds himself of his earlier resolution: 'I did never think to marry' (220), but he brushes aside his qualms with a splendid stroke of bravado.

> I may chance have some odd quirks and remnants of wit broken on me because I have railed so long against marriage. But doth not the appetite alter? A man loves the meat in his youth that he cannot endure in his age. Shall quips and sentences and these paper bullets of the brain awe a man from the career of his humour? No, the world must be peopled. When I said I would die a bachelor, I did not think I should live till I were married.
>
> (227–35)

His arguments are, of course, specious – in effect, he argues that he has changed his mind because people change their minds. In a magnificent crescendo, he declares in deadpan fashion that he is merely obeying the laws of nature. Quite selflessly, he is putting himself at the disposal of humankind, and is willing to contribute his mite towards perpetuating the human race. His parting shot is a facetious justification for his previous vow to remain a bachelor, explaining that he had assumed he would die young and hence unmarried. His soliloquy is not really an example of internal wrestling, as in later plays – Hamlet's agonizing over suicide and revenge, Brutus's attempt to rationalize the murder of a friend, Macbeth's struggle to talk himself into a course of action that goes against the fibre of his being. Instead, it is a humorous set piece, addressed to the spectators of the play. It dazzles with comic rhetorical flourishes, from Benedick's jocular metaphor comparing love to changing tastes in food, counterpoising 'love' to 'cannot endure' and 'youth' to 'age', his breezy dismissal of other men's wit at his expense by deploying the brilliant image of harmless 'paper bullets of the brain', his string of rhetorical questions, to the balanced antitheses of his final line, opposing 'die' to 'live' and 'bachelor' to 'married', turning his decision into a choice for a fuller life.

As some members of the audience would realize, in Benedick's deliberation on the issue of love and marriage, he is following a celebrated model. In Plato's dialogue named *Phaedrus*, Socrates first gives a speech critical of love, then undergoes a reversal and delivers a eulogy to love. In comically debased fashion, Benedick has experienced a similar conversion. Like the great philosopher, he winds up his reasoning with a tribute to the power of the irrational over human beings. At the end of the play, Benedick turns a deaf ear to Don Pedro's attempt to taunt him about his change of heart. He abandons all effort to justify himself by means of rational argumentation, proclaiming cheerfully, 'For man is a giddy thing, and this is my conclusion' (5.4.106–7).

Prose

Shakespeare's rhetorical training enabled him to use language to create a number of effects. One of these was, of course, to evoke aesthetic pleasure. But the range of tools he deploys also serves further purposes. In this chapter we will be taking a closer look at a few of these linguistic devices. The play is predominantly set in prose, but shifts from prose to verse contribute to a change in mood. We will also analyse some of the imagery of the play and finally briefly examine one example of how the text uses language to create character.

According to conventional wisdom, aristocratic characters speak in verse, while low-life characters speak in prose. A careful reading of early modern plays reveals that this rule of thumb is continually transgressed. *Much Ado About Nothing* might be a play with one of the highest percentages of prose (only *The Merry Wives of Windsor* contains more), but it belongs to a whole group of plays where the ratio of prose to verse is consistently high. Some of these are plays that revolve around princes and kings: *Henry IV Part I* and *II* and *Henry V*. The Prince of Wales and Sir John Falstaff converse predominantly in prose. Conversely, in other plays, such as *Richard II*, the Gardener speaks verse (as does everyone else in the play), and in *The Tempest* Caliban, the savage on the unnamed island, speaks some of the most exquisite verse lines in the play. What emerges is that the use of prose or verse in early modern drama was a stylistic choice, not a matter of set rules. Admittedly, the norm was blank verse, with rhymed verse used for specific moments such as the final lines of a scene, or for lyric forms such as songs or prologues. But even this loose set of rules is more honoured in the breach than in the observance.

It might be useful to recall that prose did not necessarily mean everyday speech. Sometimes it was more elaborate and freighted with rhetorical figures than verse. If one of the influences shaping Shakespeare's prose was euphuism, the modish technique invented by his contemporary John Lyly, abounding in parallelism, antithesis and alliteration, another important and earlier influence was Ciceronian prose, an indispensable item on the school curriculum. In Cicero's prose, rhythm played a major role, as did the equilibrium of clauses and the use of antitheses. His writing was rich in ornament and *copia*, or the repetition of statements in divergent form. His sentences were often long, and in his orations he favoured a *paratactic* syntax, that is, a parallel sequence of clauses of equal weight and importance. (The opposite would be *hypotaxis*, a hierarchical arrangement of clauses that subordinates certain ideas to others.) He was also fond of what is known as a periodic sentence, building up clauses in a sentence the syntax of which would only be resolved at the end, when the sense was completed. Shakespeare simplifies both Lyly and Cicero's style, turning prose into a far more flexible instrument that he could adapt to different purposes and divergent speakers. In the speeches of Benedick and Beatrice it is more naturalistic and sounds less pretentious than when Lyly's characters discourse. The same holds true for another pair of lovers, Rosalind and Orlando, whose flirtation in the forest of Arden in *As You Like It* takes place predominantly in prose.

A magnificent example of prose in *Much Ado About Nothing* is Benedick's outburst after being (as he thinks) mortally insulted by Beatrice during the masque. She has pointedly called him 'the prince's jester' (2.1.125), implying that he is merely a court entertainer, and not a very good one at that. Benedick volubly complains to the Prince about his mistreatment, delivering a stream of witty invective about Beatrice:

> O, she misused me past the endurance of a block! An oak but with one green leaf on it would have answered her; my very visor began to assume life and scold with her! She told me, not thinking I had been myself, that I was the prince's jester, that I was duller than a great thaw, huddling jest upon jest with such impossible conveyance upon me that I stood like a man at a mark, with a whole army shooting at me. She speaks poniards, and every word stabs. If her breath were as terrible as her terminations there were no living near her, she would infect to the North Star.
>
> (219–29)

To lend emphasis to his words, Benedick breathlessly piles on image after image. Even dead objects would find themselves stirred into life by Beatrice's verbal insults, he declares – his mask, for instance, leaps into action and defends its wearer. A finely inventive touch is the depiction of a tree that was almost dead, but not quite, being roused to defend him against her attack. He uses the simile of snow thawing at the end of the winter to express the boredom Beatrice accuses him of inspiring, and then switches to a grotesque metaphor of verbal violence, comparing Beatrice to an army shooting at him with a rapid-fire arsenal of sneers. From bullets or arrows he shifts to daggers, to which he compares her sharp words. His thoughts hurtle to the next image, drawing an analogy between her mocking language and foul breath. Her outpourings are so overwhelming that they would be capable of infecting the entire world, killing off all life in her vicinity.

His inventive, exuberant account of Beatrice's powerful tongue, mobilizing a multitude of details to produce a vivid impression of mock-physical assault, is typical of his style of wit at its most playful. As we have seen in Chapter 1, apart from comic hyperbole, his favourite device is amplification, heaping up details to reinforce the humour of his narrative. When Beatrice re-enters the stage, he simulates an urgent desire to flee, begging his Prince to send him away on a mission.

Will your grace command me any service to the world's end? I will go on the slightest errand now to the Antipodes that you can devise to send me on. I will fetch you a tooth-picker now from the furthest inch of Asia; bring you the length of Prester John's foot; fetch you a hair off the Great Cham's beard; do you any embassage to the Pygmies, rather than hold three words' conference with this harpy. You have no employment for me?

(241–9)

In a string of cleverly crafted parallel clauses, Benedick bombards Don Pedro with a barrage of absurd suggestions, each more hair-raising that the previous one. He offers to go on a quest to the Antipodes, to Asia, to the fabled Prester John in India (or, alternatively, Ethiopia), to the equally legendary ruler of China, or to the mythical Pygmies at yet another exotic location. All the adventures he proposes would involve gruelling journeys undertaken for flimsy goals – getting hold of a toothpick, of the measurements of the foot of the emperor–priest Prester John, of a hair from the Cham of China's beard. But he would be willing to do anything rather than face Beatrice, whom he adds to the sequence of fabulous persons, but as the most dangerous (and most alluring) figure – a monster with the face of a beautiful woman. His hare-brained schemes are so wildly exaggerated that they are hugely entertaining, which is precisely the effect he aims to create.

Prose and verse

Much Ado About Nothing displays a masterly command of the gradations of prose, but on occasion the play changes to verse. Leah Scragg has ingeniously suggested that the alternation from prose to verse and back again might be compared to the use of sound effects in today's performances, be it stage or screen. There is often a continuous backdrop of music in films that we no longer consciously register, but which subtly manipulates the atmosphere of a scene. For audiences carefully attuned to picking up the slightest nuances in the spoken word, as were early modern spectators, the shift from one mode to another would signal an alteration in mood. In general, blank verse was regarded as a more elevated and formal mode of speech, befitting aristocratic speakers and official scenarios. When these protagonists moved into prose, spectators would be alert to emotional upheaval in their lives – at its most extreme, in the prose sleepwalking utterances by Lady Macbeth, or the mad scenes of Ophelia. Sometimes, however, the transposition of dialogue into verse or prose served to foreground the importance of what was taking place, by analogy to dramatic background music in film. Rather than attempting to pin down characters or action to either prose or verse, it might be most helpful to observe the interplay between various registers and what they might signify.

In *Much Ado About Nothing*, the first modification takes place in Act 1 Scene 1, after Benedick has left and Claudio and Don Pedro are alone on stage. Claudio initiates a serious heart-to-heart conversation with his Prince, confessing his

marriage plans and asking for his superior's help in wooing
Hero. Appropriately, this conversation takes place in blank
verse. During the masque in Act 2 Scene 1, Claudio is the
target of malicious hearsay by Don John and Borachio, who
inform him that the Prince has wooed the woman he loves
for himself. In this emotionally charged situation, Claudio
switches to verse to articulate his grief. A more curious
case is the gulling of Beatrice, which is entirely set in verse.
By contrast, Benedick's gulling, in the scene immediately
preceding the gulling of Beatrice, is in prose. This might serve
to heighten our awareness of the subtle differences between
both scenes, despite the joint plan to make Beatrice and
Benedick fall in love with each other that both scenes are
intended to implement. In a conversation tailored to have the
maximum possible impact on the eavesdropping Benedick,
his friends concoct a story about Beatrice's passion for him,
which they recount with relish. Beatrice is described as heartbroken and madly in love to the extent that Hero fears for her
life – 'afeared that she will do a desperate outrage to herself',
as Leonato reports (2.3.150–1). What prevents Beatrice from
confessing her love is Benedick's haughty demeanour and
his contempt towards any sign of weakness on her part. The
plotters round off their narrative by tossing in a few compliments to Benedick, albeit tongue-in-cheek.

The effect that the trio of schemers have aimed for promptly
sets in. By a mixture of vanity, a sense of chivalry towards a
lady in distress and concern for Beatrice, Benedick is inspired
to change his behaviour. To a certain – but much lesser –
extent, he is shamed into reforming himself by their comments
on his high-handed manner, remarking, 'I hear how I am
censured: they say I will bear myself proudly if I perceive the
love come from her … I must not seem proud' (217–21). He
resolves to turn over a new leaf.

As regards Beatrice, the conversation of the conspiring
women takes quite a different direction. Hero's instructions
to Ursula are quite clear: 'Our talk must only be of Benedick'
(3.1.17). Ursula's brief is to praise him as an outstanding

exemplar of mankind. Hero herself will talk about how stricken he is by love-sickness. Ursula faithfully follows the script, producing the right cue by pretending to enquire, 'Doth not the gentleman / Deserve as full as fortunate a bed / As ever Beatrice shall couch upon?' (44–6). At this point Hero diverges from her scripted part. She launches into a vicious attack on Beatrice:

> But Nature never framed a woman's heart
> Of prouder stuff that that of Beatrice.
> Disdain and Scorn ride sparkling in her eyes,
> Misprising what they look on, and her wit
> Values itself so highly that to her
> All matter else seems weak. She cannot love,
> Nor take no shape nor project of affection,
> She is so self-endeared.
>
> (49–56)

Her cousin, she claims, is puffed up with self-importance and arrogance. Hero uses personifications for 'Disdain' and 'Scorn', but it is clear that she is alluding to Beatrice. Fully conscious of her superior intelligence, Beatrice regards all other mortals with scorn and contempt. In a final blow, Hero labels Beatrice as someone who is so enamoured of herself that she is incapable of feeling love for others. And Hero does not stop at this point. She embarks on another speech deriding Beatrice for her critical response to an assortment of men to whom she has been introduced. None of them, it seems, were to her liking. Ursula hastens to add a placatory 'Sure, sure, such carping is not commendable' (71), only for Hero to carry on her diatribe: 'No, not to be so odd and from all fashions / As Beatrice is cannot be commendable' (72–3).

One might gain the impression that Hero has approached the heart of the matter. The source of her resentment against her vivacious cousin, whose effervescent wit has left her in the shadow throughout the play, is that Beatrice dares to break the mould of conventional feminine behaviour. Indeed, Hero hints that she is unnatural – Nature has never created a woman like her. Beatrice is an individualist and a non-conformist, which on Hero's terms is 'odd' and 'from all fashions'. Beatrice stands for the diametrical opposite of everything Hero represents. If norms for Renaissance womanhood are based on the triad of being chaste, silent and obedient, Beatrice fulfils only one of the three behavioural precepts. There is no question that she is chaste, but silence and obedience are disciplines that she is happy to leave to Hero. Indeed, in an earlier scene she even encourages her companion to be somewhat more assertive about her own desires. When their uncle, Antonio, reminds his niece with regard to her marriage, 'I trust you will be ruled by your father', Beatrice throws in, 'it is my cousin's duty to make curtsy, and say, "Father, as it please you." But yet for all that, cousin, let him be a handsome fellow, or else make another curtsy, and say, "Father, as it please me"' (2.1.46–9). In jocular manner, Beatrice is urging Hero to take charge of her own life and demand that her own wishes be taken into account in as momentous a decision as one touching on her future as wife. Hero, characteristically, remains silent.

In the gulling scene, Hero is hard put to rein in her tongue. Deviating entirely from the original plan, she broods on her own relationship to Beatrice. She is afraid to confront her cousin directly. 'If I should speak / She would mock me into air. O, she would laugh me / Out of myself, press me to death with wit!' (3.1.74–6), she exclaims. Her rancour against the free-spirited Beatrice finds expression in the barbaric metaphor she deploys, one that is quite uncalled for in the light-hearted context of the scene. Pressing someone to death with heavy weights was a form of torture meted out to prisoners who refused to confess or speak out as desired by the authorities. Hero laments the dilemma she finds herself in in relation to Beatrice. Should she attempt to give voice to her thoughts, she fears, she would receive endless ridicule at the hands of her far more articulate cousin. Nothing in the play bears out any of these insinuations. Whenever we see Hero and Beatrice together, we observe a solicitous if slightly patronizing response to Hero on Beatrice's part, unsullied by a note of envy or malice. In point of fact, at the catastrophic wedding, Beatrice emerges as the most loyal supporter Hero has, leaving her father and uncle far behind.

Returning briefly to her script, Hero devises a tale of Benedick's love-sickness, but then she makes a further surprising detour. The Prince and his companions end their fictive account of Beatrice's suffering inconclusively, hoping to stir Benedick's pity and sense of gallantry and hence set him on the path of wooing Beatrice. The plan succeeds admirably. Hero, on the other hand, announces decisively, 'I will go to Benedick / And counsel him to fight against his passion. / And truly, I'll devise some honest slanders / To stain my cousin with' (82–6). The oxymoronic term 'honest slanders' is one of the most ironic that the play has to offer, all the more so since 'honest' referred to 'honour', a key ideological tool employed in the attack against Hero later in the play. It is linked to the undercurrent of irony that runs through the play. Hero's earlier remarks about Beatrice's eyes '[M]isprising what they look on' strikes a further ironic note. The play is saturated with examples of misprision, but the victim of the disdain and scorn of the citizens of Messina, as of their poisonous words, is Hero herself. The psychological torment she undergoes leaves her in a state of metaphorical death, but she is mistaken in associating Beatrice with the pain inflicted on her.

Even the usually compliant Ursula is alarmed at Hero's spiteful words. She protests, 'O, do not do your cousin such a wrong!' (87). Both intriguers revert to the plan outlined at the beginning of the scene and devote themselves to lavishing praise on Benedick. When they leave, Beatrice comes forward to hold a brief soliloquy. This, too, deviates from the final speech delivered by Benedick in subtle ways. It bears citing in full.

What fire is in mine ears? Can this be true?
Stand I condemned for pride and scorn so much?
Contempt, farewell; and maiden pride, adieu;
No glory lives behind the back of such.

And Benedick, love on. I will requite thee,
Taming my wild heart to thy loving hand.
If thou dost love, my kindness shall incite thee
To bind our loves up in a holy band.
For others say thou dost deserve, and I
Believe it better than reportingly.

(107–16)

Beatrice's soliloquy takes the form of a truncated sonnet, which in the English mode of sonnets usually contains fourteen lines of iambic pentameter. Iambic pentameter consists of ten syllables in each line, with the stress lying on every second syllable. By contrast, Beatrice's speech contains twelve lines, with two extra syllables in two lines, each pointedly ending on the word 'thee' (11, 13) and a jagged, asymmetrical metre in the line sandwiched between them: 'Tàming my wìld heàrt to thy lòving hànd' (14). All three lines disrupt the norm of iambic pentameter. The line beginning with the word 'Taming' is the only line to start on a stressed syllable, or a *trochee*. The word is further highlighted through an internal rhyme in the same sentence – it is echoed by 'loving'. It is almost as if Beatrice is fully aware of how huge a step she is taking when she vows to change her behaviour. And the metrical dissonance cannot fail to strike a careful listener in the early modern age, accustomed as they were to hear the nuances at work in the modish genre of the sonnet. For Beatrice, allowing herself to embark on a relationship of love and marriage exacts a far higher toll than for Benedick. The cost involved is a loss of freedom and self-determination, all the more so as early modern marriage conventions that expected women to be submissive to their husbands were cemented in the subordinate legal status of married women.

The structural similarities between the two gulling scenes is undermined by the permutation from prose to verse. The impact of the scenes on the two maverick characters, Beatrice and Benedick, is quite different. For Benedick, it is a matter of accepting the love of a woman whom his friends claim is passionately in love with him, and to whom he has long been attracted. The main strategy employed to trap him into an alliance with a member of the opposite sex has been flattery and an appeal to his vanity. In the case of Beatrice, the critique she has been made to hear is far harsher. She stands condemned for having a supercilious and contemptuous personality. She hears a scathing judgement about her boundless self-absorption, which allegedly makes her incapable of entering into bonds with other human beings. The devastating assessment of her character is not put forward by those who dislike her, but by her nearest and dearest relative, with whom she shares the intimacy of a bedchamber. As a result, her self-esteem is dealt a crippling blow. She struggles to regain equilibrium and resolves to reform herself – a resolve that she takes far more seriously than Benedick, and one that will cost her far more in terms of pride and self-respect. She offers to tame herself, to voluntarily rein in her independent nature. Her cousin aptly describes her as 'coy and wild / As haggards of the rock' (35–6), comparing her wariness of close contact to other human beings to that of wild hawks. Hawks were traditionally admired as birds of prey and used in the aristocratic art of falconry. But unlike other beasts with whom early moderns had close relations in the sport of hunting, they were acknowledged to remain alien to humans in spirit, despite the close rapport that evolved between hunter and hawk.

To be sure, Benedick too pays a high price for his decision. Unlike Claudio, he strives for a union of mutuality and trust with the woman he loves. When the couple finally confess their attraction to each other, Beatrice makes a drastic demand of her lover: to kill his closest companion, Claudio. As will be discussed in Chapter 3, Benedick abandons not only his former companions, but his patron and source of employment, Don Pedro, and rejects the very code of honour they embody. Bonds of reciprocity between men and women in Shakespeare's plays repeatedly call on both parts to sacrifice their intimate friendships with members of their own sex – a tension that, as the critic Carol Thomas Neely points out, might lie at the heart of the cuckoldry jokes particularly male characters are so fond of cracking. Humour often serves as a social corrective, re-inforcing norms and mocking deviants. Cuckoldry jokes tap into anxieties about losing face, a particularly potent fear in a culture that was in the grip of notions of honour that regarded women as male possessions whose conduct reflected on men's reputation. Sometimes, however, these jokes served other purposes. As we have seen, their main function could be to strengthen male solidarity. But laughter at these quips could also work as a coping strategy for both sides. In Shakespeare's comedies, women like Rosalind and Portia jest about being unfaithful to their husbands and making cuckolds of them. Jesting was a time-honoured device in the battle of the sexes and gave expression to the contradictory forces of desire and fear – the apprehensiveness of both men and women about losing their independence and entering into a relationship with members of the opposite sex. Humour was frequently conducive to defusing these tensions.

Perhaps the shift in registers from prose to verse in the two gulling scenes of otherwise striking symmetry might contribute towards foregrounding the hidden differences between the gulling of Benedick and that of Beatrice. In the rest of the play, reasons that might be adduced for the transition from prose to verse and vice versa are far more straightforward. Throughout, the mutations of mode heighten the dramatic effect. The church scene, the climax of the entire play, is in verse, as befits not only the solemn setting, but the sombre mood that overcasts the play from this point onwards. The declaration of love between Beatrice and Benedick, by contrast, which initiates a new, crucial development in the plot, is marked by transposing it into the key of prose. Verse is used for sequences of dialogue that have tragic overtones, such as Leonato's grief at the fate of his child and his threat of revenge in Act 5 Scene 1. When Don Pedro and Claudio are alone on stage, they jeer at the two impotent old men, Leonato and Antonio, and attempt to horse around with Benedick as in old times – in prose.

But once Dogberry enters with his charges and they hear Borachio's confession, they shift back into verse. The final scene of the play, with the nuptials between the masked women and their suitors, is couched in verse – until, that is, the reluctance of Beatrice and Benedick to enter into the state of matrimony is overcome by means of the comic device of waving their own poetic effusions under their nose. The play dissolves into joyous revelry and throws poetry overboard for prose.

Imagery

Imagery – which includes figurative language, especially similes and metaphor, as well as literal images evoked in descriptive language – is a useful tool to reinforce the potency of language. Some of the most interesting effects, however, are created when the imagery a character uses inadvertently pulls against the message he or she is trying to convey. A few examples should suffice to demonstrate this device in action.

The plotters, aiming to trick Benedick and Beatrice into falling 'into a mountain of affection' with each other (2.1.338), consistently use a vocabulary of ensnaring birds and beasts for their scheme. Many of their comments are asides or remarks directed at the audience, which serve to heighten our enjoyment of the scenario unfolding before us by making us feel complicit in the conspiracy. Benedick believes he is well hidden from his friends, not realizing that they are pursuing him as a prey to be hunted. Claudio gleefully remarks to his co-conspirators, 'We'll fit the kid-fox with a pennyworth', comparing Benedick to a fox cub with whom they will drive a hard bargain (2.3.40). When Don Pedro launches into a fictive account of Beatrice's passion for Benedick, Claudio encourages him, saying 'stalk on, stalk on, the fowl sits' (94), this time referring to their victim as a game bird. Later, he remarks to Don Pedro, 'Bait the hook well, this fish will bite!' (110), switching to the idiom of fishing. Convinced of their success, Don Pedro urges his companions to continue the prank by practising it on Beatrice: 'Let there be the same net spread for her' (206–7). In the parallel scene, now aimed at entrapping Beatrice, Hero and Ursula first describe their victim in terms of a bird, then move to the imagery of fishing, just as Claudio did in the previous scenario. As Hero explains, they are laying a 'false-sweet bait' (3.1.33) for Beatrice, enticing her into love by means of lies. When Beatrice creeps up behind them to overhear their conversation, having been lured to the orchard by Margaret, Hero compares her to a fowl, observing, 'For look where Beatrice like a lapwing runs / Close by the ground to hear our conference' (3.1.24–5). The lapwing or plover was a ground-nesting bird, often associated with female deceit (McEachern 2016: 259). Ironically, while both Benedick and Beatrice assume they are practising a fraud on their companions by eavesdropping on their conversation, it is they themselves who are the dupes.

Ursula perceives the analogy between the trickery of Beatrice and the catching of fish. 'The pleasant'st angling is to see the fish / Cut with her golden oars the silver stream / And greedily devour the treacherous bait', she notes, adding, 'So angle we for Beatrice' (26–9). A somewhat jarring note is sounded with the term 'treacherous', preparing us for Hero's slander of her cousin in the ensuing dialogue. At the end of the scene, Ursula reverts to the comparison to ensnaring birds, gleefully promising her mistress, 'She's limed, I warrant you! We have caught her, madam!' (104). Birdlime was an adhesive substance spread on branches to catch birds. The entire field of imagery is not particularly original in relation to practical jokes, although the baited fish are described in surprisingly aesthetic terms, as shimmering golden while swimming in silver water. Far more interesting are Hero's initial remarks with regard to the first part of the hoax, made before Beatrice's entrance. She instructs Margaret to decoy Beatrice to the orchard by inventing a tale about having overheard Hero and Ursula talk about her. Margaret is to insinuate that Beatrice might be able to eavesdrop on the conversation herself.

> Say that thou overheard'st us,
> And bid her steal into the pleached bower
> Where honeysuckles ripened by the sun
> Forbid the sun to enter, like favourites
> Made proud by princes that advance their pride
> Against that power that bred it; there will she hide her
> To listen our propose.
>
> (6–12)

This attractive pastoral locale, an arbour screened by inter-twining ('pleached') branches of honeysuckle vine, is delineated in strange terms. Hero speaks of climbing plants that require sunlight to flourish, but which have spread to the extent that they now shut out the sun. She draws an analogy to courtiers whose careers have been supported by a ruler, but who turn rebellious and attempt to challenge the power of the prince. There is no conclusion to her simile; one assumes that the presumptuous noblemen will be punished, but there is no mention of this in the narrative. The imagery she uses is unusual. She might be alluding to her cousin, Beatrice, whom she seems to regard as analogous to a court favourite, having been permitted to grow unchecked by the powerful people in her environment – a possible reference to the patriarch, Leonato, whom we have seen in Act 2 Scene 1, fondly lenient towards his niece while laying strict injunctions on his daughter. At the same time, the proud plants seem to be thriving, and have created an idyllic world from which the sun, the source of power, is excluded. The image resonates with a mixture of resentment, envy and admiration for her self-confident cousin. As Harry Berger, Jr, points out, the metaphor of majestic honeysuckles works to undermine the point Hero seems to be trying to make, censuring both the plants and, by association, her proud cousin (2001: 18–19). However, the image is ambiguous, and might hint at Hero's own revolt against the powerful influence of Beatrice. Interestingly, the pastoral locations in the play are consistently associated with duplicity and surveillance. The first eavesdropping scenario, during which Don Pedro and Claudio were overheard conversing about their plan for the Prince to woo Hero by proxy for Claudio by a servant of Antonio's, took place in another 'thick-pleached alley' in Antonio's orchard (1.2.8), while Benedick imagined he was spying on his friends in an orchard, too. Needless to say, in Christian mythology the pastoral as a site for treachery reaches back to the beginning of time.

Controlling metaphor

The cardinal metaphor of the play concerns the notion of fashion. Allusions to fashion run through *Much Ado About Nothing* like a contrapuntal theme. The very first act of the play abounds in incidental mentions of the term. These have been discussed in the Introduction, but a brief recapitulation might be helpful. In the opening scene, Beatrice scathingly comments that Benedick 'wears his faith but as the fashion of his hat: it ever changes with the next block' (1.1.70–2). His loyalties are as fickle as his taste in hats. In the same scene, Don Pedro greets Leonato with exquisite polish, saying, 'Good Signor Leonato, are you come to meet your trouble? The fashion of the world is to avoid cost, and you encounter it' (91–3). Benedick scoffs at his friends, whose attempt to compete with him in the discipline of wit falls woefully flat. The metaphor he utilizes is from the field of fashion: 'The body of your discourse is sometime guarded with fragments, and the guards are but slightly basted on neither' (266–8). What he is referring to is the dressmaker's bodice, ornamented with trimmings ('guards'), which are only loosely sewn on. Similarly, Don Pedro and Claudio have picked up scraps of wit that they are trying out on Benedick, but the effect is ragtag and unconvincing. Don John bitterly remarks that he prefers being ostracized by society to having to 'fashion a carriage to rob love from any' (1.3.27). He is loath to adopt the smooth manners fashionable at court in order to ingratiate himself with the charmed circle around his brother. The speakers all use the term 'fashion' in divergent senses, but the play sets up a series of echoes that reverberate far into the action. And all refer to outward forms of behaviour or the impressions created by surface manifestations.

As in the remark by Don John, one set of references to 'fashion' points specifically to the manipulation of impressions. When Don Pedro first moots the idea of duping Benedick and Beatrice into falling in love, he boasts, 'I doubt not to fashion it' (2.1.340). This is immediately followed by a scene in which Borachio proposes a plot against Claudio, catering to a desire voiced by Don John to harm the close associate of his brother in every possible way. It is noteworthy that the expression Borachio uses echoes Don Pedro's precise words: 'I will so fashion the matter', he promises Don John (2.2.42–3). The verbal parallels highlight the striking affinities between the brothers, despite their overt antagonism. Another stage manager figure, Friar Francis, uses the same term in connection with the plan he has conceived to save the honour of Hero. By simulating that she has died through shock, he proposes, Claudio will be struck by remorse and regret his brutal behaviour to her. 'Let this be so, and doubt not but success / Will fashion the event in better shape / Than I can lay it down in likelihood' (4.1.234–6), he promises, foreseeing an even more favourable outcome of events than he dare predict.

Another cluster of observations bears explicitly upon the cult of modish behaviour and clothes with which early modern society was preoccupied. Benedick laments that he no longer recognizes his compeer, Claudio, on whom he bestows the nickname 'Monsieur Love' (2.3.34). He reminisces,

I have known when there was no music with him but the drum and the fife, and now had he rather hear the tabor and the pipe. I have known when he would have walked

ten mile afoot to see a good armour, and now will he lie
ten nights awake carving the fashion of a new doublet. He
was wont to speak plain and to the purpose, like an honest
man and a soldier, now is he turned orthography; his words
are a very fantastical banquet, just so many strange dishes.
May I be so converted and see with these eyes?

(2.3.12–22)

Benedick mourns the loss of a life of martial simplicity that he
shared with his comrade – ironically, in polished, measured
prose. Claudio's taste in music, dress and even language has
undergone a radical change. No longer does he delight in
military marches, well-crafted armour and straightforward
speech. Instead, he is now immersed in social life, smart
clothes and elegant conversation. From a soldier he has
now been transformed into a dedicated follower of fashion.
Benedick puts forward these thoughts in typically waggish
manner – but it is hardly the wooden, tongue-tied Claudio
who strikes us as having 'turned orthography', but Benedick
himself, with his hyperbolical, vivid prose.

Don Pedro confirms Benedick's view about Claudio's fascination with dashing attire. When Claudio offers to accompany
his prince immediately after the wedding, Don Pedro rejects
the offer, insisting that his newlywed friend should not
be bereft of the joys of marriage so soon after the event.
Significantly, the analogy that springs to his mind is one from
the realm of fashion: 'that would be as great a soil in the new
gloss of your marriage as to show a child his new coat and
forbid him to wear it' (3.2.5–7). Clearly, Don Pedro considers
a comparison to the pleasure of new clothes to be an ideal
description of the bliss of honeymoon.

As it happens, Claudio is not the only person in the play
absorbed in natty apparel. Don Pedro and Claudio team up to
tease Benedick about his extravagant style, borrowing fashions
generously from all corners of the earth: 'a Dutchman today,
a Frenchman tomorrow – or in the shape of two countries at
once, as a German from the waist downward, all slops, and a

Spaniard from the hip upward, no doublet' (3.2.31–4). They rib him mercilessly about his visit to the barber's, his lavish use of perfume and the cosmetics he has applied – signs, they claim, that he is in love. All of Messina is caught up in a frenzy of fashion.

While dressing the bride for the wedding, Margaret keeps up an animated flow of fashion patter, describing a dress of the Duchess of Milan for our benefit: 'cloth o' gold, and cuts, and laced with silver, set with pearls, down sleeves, side sleeves, and skirts round underborne with a bluish tinsel' (3.4.18–20). When Leonato and his brother Antonio encounter the Prince and Claudio after Hero's reputation has been shattered by their accusation, Antonio taunts them as being dandified swaggerers:

Scrambling, outfacing, fashion-mongering boys,
That lie, and cog, and flout, deprave, and slander,
Go anticly and show outward hideousness,
And speak off half a dozen dangerous words
How they might hurt their enemies, if they durst –
(5.1.94–8).

Antonio believes that for these stylish young men, lying, cheating and defaming others go hand in hand with the absurd fashions they sport. However, as he insinuates, their courage lies merely in a brazen show of aggression and in boasts of violence, not in actual feats. The fashionable youths are all show and no substance.

The society of Messina is not exceptional in its worship of fashion. In the sixteenth century the English were frequently mocked for their mania for fashion, a term that gained its present connotations in this period (*OED* 10). A burgeoning consumer industry made an assortment of costly fabrics available to whoever could afford them – the sumptuary laws that regulated which social rank was permitted to wear certain materials were so widely flouted that they soon became defunct. Distinctions of dress were no longer reliable as a benchmark of social status. Clothes were possibly the most exorbitant item in a society that increasingly set a premium on conspicuous consumption (Newman 1991). Some aristocrats spent over half their annual budget on acquiring new apparel, and there was an explosion of plays on stage that satirized social climbers who bankrupted themselves trying to ape the dress of the more affluent members of society, while the merchant class grew wealthy catering to the new taste for luxury goods. While social critics such as Philip Stubbes in *The Anatomie of Abuses* (1836 [1585]), roundly castigated sartorial prodigality, sales in clothes, even at secondhand, expanded to an unprecedented degree (Jones and Stallybrass 2000).

The most pointed reference in the play to the cult of fashion appears in a set piece by the tipsy Borachio shortly before his arrest. Boasting to Conrade of his part in the plot to trick Claudio and the Prince into believing Hero is disloyal, he launches into a long-winded diatribe against fashion.

> Seest thou not, I say, what a deformed thief this fashion is, how giddily 'a turns about all the hot-bloods between fourteen and five-and-thirty, sometimes fashioning them like Pharaoh's soliders in the reechy painting, sometimes like god Bel's priests in the old church window, sometime like the shaven Hercules in the smirched worm-eaten tapestry, where his cod-piece seems as massy as his club.
>
> (3.3.126–33)

Borachio is drunk and his words are almost as much a farrago of sense and nonsense as is the speech of Dogberry and consorts. What is clear, however, is that he regards fashion, or external show, as 'deformed' (or rather, deforming) – it warps the truth. Everyone, he complains, is in thrall to an obsession with fashion. His allusions to a hoary past are a snarl of historical and mythological references, and it is not quite clear what he means. All the examples he cites are, however, victims of deception. In the Book of Exodus in the Old Testament, the Egyptian army in pursuit of the Israelites was drowned in the

Red Sea. In another story, Bel and the Dragon (an addition to the Old Testament book of Daniel that Roman Catholic and Orthodox Christians accept as canonical), the prophet Daniel exposed the priests of the Sumerian god Baal (Bel) as frauds who tricked the king into worshipping a dead idol. The Greek hero Hercules was often depicted with a huge club, but the reference to his being shaven seems to be a jumbled-up version of the myth of Hercules and Omphale, an Oriental queen whom the hero was made to serve as a slave for a year. The tale was embellished with accounts of Omphale forcing the great hero to commit labour usually consigned to women, and even dressing him in female clothes. Hence the detail about the 'shaven' Hercules would imply that in the story he had been deprived of all emblems of his masculinity, including his beard, but in the depiction on the tapestry Borachio mentions, Hercules' prominent codpiece suggests a virility that was deceptive. Interestingly, all stories relate to devotees of idolatry, as were ancient Egyptians, the priests of the idol Baal and the Greeks of antiquity, and two of the narratives derive from dubious sources – the aforementioned additions to the Book of Daniel about Baal (Bel) were rejected by Protestants as apocryphal, later additions, while the legend of Hercules seems to be conflated with the story of Samson and Delilah in the Old Testament, where Samson loses his power once he has been divested of his hair. Borachio's gesturing at depictions in paintings, stained glass windows in churches and tapestries reinforces the connotations of idolatry, and his contemptuous descriptions of these illustrations as 'reechy' and 'smirched' (or grimy), 'old' and 'worm-eaten' add to the layers pointing to the untrustworthiness of appearances.

Borachio goes on to reveal to Conrade how Claudio and Don Pedro have been hoodwinked into believing that Hero is unfaithful. He and Margaret, Hero's gentlewoman-in-waiting, have played an erotic game of make-believe in which each takes on the role of their social superiors, Claudio and Hero. The Prince and Hero's fiancé, eavesdropping on the scene, are fully persuaded that they are witnesses to Hero's infidelity, and draw conclusions accordingly. And the oafish watchmen, who for their part have been eavesdropping on Borachio and Conrade, produce their own distorted version of this conversation, and are convinced that they have uncovered a conspiracy by a thief named Deformed who appears in the guise of a gentleman: 'I know that Deformed', one of the watchmen exclaims: ''A has been a vile thief this seven year; 'a goes up and down like a gentleman' (121–3). In the heavily embroidered version later furnished by the play's arch buffoon, Dogberry, this fantasy character has metamorphosed further, and is now described as wearing a key and lock dangling from his ear in a sly punning mutation from love-lock to padlock. Fashion, personified as a thief by Borachio, has now been transposed into a would-be gallant, complete with earring, who apes the manners of his betters. As the clowns collectively suspect, he is trying to steal his way into fashionable society. In their conservative judgement, social mobility is a far more heinous crime than is slandering a gentlewoman. The central metaphor of fashion subsumes some of the dominant concerns of the play – appearance and reality, style and issues of social rank.

Character

Language is used by Shakespeare to create character not only in terms of what the protagonists of the play say, but in the way in which they express themselves – and what they never say. In the space remaining, we will take a brief look at only one character, Claudio. As noted in the Introduction, Shakespeare made a number of significant changes to his source material, some of which have a bearing on the depiction of Claudio.

When we first encounter Claudio, he is pondering his choice of a bride. Not able or willing to trust his own judgement, he is anxious to canvass the opinions of his peers. He needles his companion, Benedick, to tell him what he thinks of her. Exasperated, Benedick responds, 'Would you buy her that you inquire after her?' (1.1.170). He is not wide of the mark. Even though Claudio counters with a rhetorical question, exclaiming sententiously, 'Can the world buy such a jewel?' (171), in truth, for Claudio, Hero figures in the marriage market as a valuable commodity that he is anxious to acquire. When alone with his mentor, the Prince, he pursues this line of enquiry. He wishes to know whether Leonato has a son. Don Pedro correctly infers that his query aims at the fortune Hero will inherit, and confirms that she is her father's only heir (275–6). Only then does Claudio embark on a little speech about how, now that the war is over and he has leisure at his disposal, he has fallen in love: 'But now I am returned, and that war-thoughts / Have left their places vacant, in their rooms / Come thronging soft and delicate desires, / All prompting me how fair young Hero is' (282–6). The lines, like most of his speeches, are couched in clichéd commonplaces. Don Pedro broaches his plan to woo Hero in Claudio's guise and then hand her over to his friend. Not a word of protest passes Claudio's lips. For him, his bonds with Don Pedro are paramount – they have engaged in the wars together, and will undertake their amorous ventures together.

During the first few scenes of the play, Don John and his henchmen follow no coherent plan, but merely aim to stir up discord between Don Pedro and his closest companion. When they come across Claudio during the masque, they inform him that the Prince is wooing Hero for himself. Without taking a moment to reflect, Claudio immediately falls victim to the piece of misinformation he has been fed – a consistent mode of behaviour we see repeated the second time he is offered a manipulated version of the truth. His soliloquy is revealing.

'Tis certain so; the prince woos for himself.
Friendship is constant in all other things,
Save in the office and affairs of love.
Therefore all hearts in love use their own tongues:
Let every eye negotiate for itself,

And trust no agent; for Beauty is a witch
Against whose charms faith melteth into blood.
This is an accident of hourly proof
Which I mistrusted not. Farewell, therefore, Hero!

(2.1.159–67)

Convinced of the truth of the idea planted by Don John, Claudio blames himself for trusting his friend to woo in his place. Then he moves on to draw a startling conclusion: it is the beauty of women – and, by extension, of Hero herself – that is to blame. Male loyalty is impotent in the face of seductive female wiles. The personification he uses evokes the mythological figure of Circe, a witch whose allure trapped men on her island and whose power transformed them into beasts. Not a breath of reproach for Don Pedro passes Claudio's lips. Instead, he makes haste to free himself from the spell cast by Hero. The misunderstanding is soon cleared up, but the speech uncovers the pattern that determines Claudio's personality. In his profoundly misogynist worldview, women are inherently deceitful temptresses who threaten the true ties of male friendship.

Accordingly, when the second insinuation against Hero is set in motion by Don John, Claudio has no hesitation in taking the bait. Even before he has viewed the forged evidence, he announces with a certain satisfaction, 'If I see anything tonight why I should not marry her, tomorrow in the congregation where I should wed, there will I shame her' (3.2.111–13). Claudio has not had a good press with critics. They point out that there is no hint of anguish on his part, as with Othello, or even a demand for 'ocular proof'. By contrast, Claudio seems to be relishing the thought of a betrayal by the woman he says he loves and is keen to plan a spectacular public revenge. It is his eagerness to leap to conclusions that has made critics like Betrand Evans label him the 'most insufferable of Shakespeare's heroes of comedy, combining the hero's usual oblivion with priggish egocentricity' (211).

The church scene is Claudio's great moment. He stages the shaming of his fiancée with military precision. After Friar

Francis delivers the ritual preliminary remarks, enquiring of the assembly whether there be any impediments to the match, Claudio takes over.

CLAUDIO
Stand thee by, Friar. [*to* LEONATO] Father, by your leave:
Will you with free and unconstrained soul
Give me this maid, your daughter?
LEONATO
As freely, son, as God did give her me.
CLAUDIO
And what have I to give you back whose worth
May counterpoise this rich and precious gift?
DON PEDRO
Nothing, unless you render her again.
CLAUDIO
Sweet Prince, you learn me noble thankfulness.
There, Leonato, take her back again.
Give not this rotten orange to your friend:
She's but the sign and semblance of her honour.

(4.1.21–31)

Assisted by Don Pedro, Claudio puts on a little charade intended to humiliate not only his bride, but his future father-in-law. He goes through the motions of accepting Hero from the hand of her father only to heighten the dramatic impact of his act of rejection. In a rhetorical query, he pretends he is musing how to show his gratitude to Leonato, overwhelmed by the richness of the present he has just received. As no doubt previously agreed, Don Pedro puts in a word, pointing out that nothing could balance the value of Hero, unless it were to return her. This provides Claudio with his own cue. An apparently mock-modest demurral to accept too precious a gift is swiftly transposed into its converse: a ferocious repudiation of the union on the grounds of fraudulence. Hero, Claudio claims, bears only the outward appearance of chastity. To underline his point he uses an alliterative *hendiadys*, a rhetorical figure in which two similar terms are linked together for emphasis where one would adequately convey the intended meaning: 'sign and semblance'. There is also a subtle jibe at Leonato's social rank, which is not as elevated as that of his future son-in-law – Claudio takes care to slip in a reference to 'noble' behaviour and to 'honour', the key defining mark of an aristocrat. Claudio's most shocking line is the degrading reference to Hero as a 'rotten orange', as if she were literally tainted goods.

Claudio proceeds with his jeremiad, gesturing towards Hero as a prize exhibit to demonstrate the moral point he is driving home. 'Behold how like a maid she blushes here! / O, what authority and show of truth / Can cunning sin cover itself withal!', he lectures his audience (32–4). The theme of his discourse is the treacherous power of appearances. Hero might appear to be blushing in shame. But, he declares apodictically, 'Her blush is guiltiness, not modesty' (40). Claudio is in his element as sermonizer. 'Out on thee, seeming!', he expostulates histrionically, attacking both the abstract notion of deceit and the concrete example of Hero, and goes on to promise his audience, 'I will write against it' (55).

After an inquisitorial examination of the accused, Claudio wraps up the case. His summation radiates sanctimonious pomposity.

> O Hero! What a Hero hadst thou been
> If half thy outward graces had been placed
> About thy thoughts and counsels of thy heart!
> But fare thee well, most foul, most fair. Farewell
> Thou pure impiety and impious purity.
>
>   (100–4)

He laments that Hero does not possess the inward beauty proclaimed by her outward appearance. His oratory becomes increasingly rich in rhetorical figures – in these few lines, he manages to insert an *apostrophe* to Hero, *alliteration*, *antonyms* and *epanalepsis* (the repetition of the same words at the beginning and at the end of a clause, here 'fare thee well' and 'Farewell'). In his last line, in addition to *chiasmus*, he throws in a handful of *oxymora* ('pure impiety' is juxtaposed with 'impious purity'), a figure of speech in which words that appear contradictory are yoked together to create a new, paradoxical meaning. By amassing rhetorical devices in Claudio's lines, Shakespeare effectively disperses any sympathy one might retain for him as the victim of betrayal, however imaginary. His speech sounds too polished to be the expression of heartbroken emotions. He is enjoying himself far too much.

Little in the rest of the play serves to redeem Claudio, despite the happy ending. When Friar Francis proposes his own scheme to salvage Hero's reputation and possibly her marriage by simulating her death, his rationale is grounded upon human nature. We tend to value things more after we have lost them, he argues. Similarly, once Claudio hears of Hero's ostensible demise, his memories of her will reawaken, and he will begin to think about her with nostalgic wistfulness. Indeed, she will become even more attractive to him in retrospect than while she was alive. 'Then shall he mourn – / If ever love had interest in his liver – / And wish he had not so accused her; / No, though he thought his accusation true' (230–3). The Friar predicts that Claudio will begin to regret his denunciation of her, even if he is still convinced of the truth of his accusations.

There is no sign of the Friar being right in his conjecture. In Act 5 Scene 1 the Prince and Claudio are challenged by Leonato and his brother, Antonio. They refuse to engage with the old men, and attempt to brush them off. When Benedick appears, the two young men amusedly recount their close shave with the two aging revengers. 'We had liked to have had our two noses snapped off with two old men without teeth', Claudio scoffs (5.1.115–16). Despite the fact that Hero is not really dead, the grief of the two old men that we have just witnessed is moving in its intensity. Claudio's tasteless remark and his demand that Benedick entertain him and

Don Pedro and help lift their spirits seem particularly callous against the backdrop of the near-tragedy he has initiated. Admittedly, once he hears Borachio's confession, he responds to the revelation of the truth with distress. He offers Leonato to do penance, willing to accept any conditions that the latter might impose. He does indeed acquiesce to Leonato's plan without demurral, promising to marry Antonio's fictive daughter who purportedly resembles Hero. Leonato, however, now seems to have the measure of his future son-in-law. He takes care to point out that the mysterious substitute for Hero is the heir to the fortune of both himself and Antonio (280). By contrast, money is never an issue in the wooing between Benedick and Beatrice. Claudio accepts the offer of a new bride with alacrity. He carries out the rites of mourning at the alleged tomb of Hero with due solemnity and contrition. Nevertheless, he insists throughout that he remains largely innocent of the near-tragic trajectory the play has taken: 'Yet sinned I not / But in mistaking' (263–4).

Writing matters

In this chapter we have sketched a few ways in which to analyse the language of the play. Here are a number of sugges-tions as to ideas worth pursuing.

1   In our discussion of the play's structure, we have only very briefly touched upon symmetrical patterns and what they might tell us. Look for further symmetries between scenes or events.

2   Look for other set pieces of prose in the play and analyse them carefully, trying to detect the rhetorical figures at work and what effects they create.

3   Look at the alternation between prose and verse in other scenes in the play and try to examine what effect the shift from one mode to another produces. You

might be interested in scrutinizing this effect in other plays as well. What is the effect of prose in the sleep-walking scene of *Macbeth*, or the scene of Ophelia's madness in *Hamlet*?

4 Do you detect patterns of imagery other than those we have discussed? One lead might be to follow further references taken from the world of animals in the play. Another suggestion would be to look at the imagery of violence – characters speak of torture, burning at the stake, poison, plague, all in a jesting manner. See if you can trace these allusions. In which way are they significant?

5 Can you think of further ways in which fashion plays a central role in the language of the play, perhaps in less direct allusions?

6 Attempt a comprehensive analysis of other characters of the play, focusing on their language. Once again, what is helpful is to look not only at what they say, but how they say it, and where they remain silent. Silence is a form of communication, too. Look, for instance, at moments where Hero is voluble, and where she is silent.

7 Look at the rhetorical strategy of arguing on both sides of an issue in other plays, focusing on soliloquies: Brutus musing whether to kill his friend in *Julius Caesar*, or Macbeth agonizing about whether to commit murder, or Hamlet considering whether to commit suicide. Are these really open-ended debates, or is the outcome a foregone conclusion?

8 Compare Claudio to other callow young protagonists in Shakespeare's plays – Bassanio in *The Merchant of Venice*, Bertram in *All's Well Ends Well*, Proteus in *The Two Gentlemen of Verona*, or Posthumus in *Cymbeline*. How are they similar, and how do they differ?

CHAPTER THREE

Language through time

Romance

Much Ado About Nothing has become famous for the relationship between Beatrice and Benedick, which is remarkable for its portrayal of two independent-minded characters who nevertheless evince a strong attraction to each other. The characters were so popular that apparently the play was often referred to solely by their names. According to court records, it was one of the plays staged during the wedding festivities of Princess Elizabeth, the eldest daughter of King James I, and Frederick V, Count Palatine of the Rhine, in 1613 under the title *Benedict and Beatrice*. Charles I noted down this alternative title next to the play in his copy of the Second Folio of Shakespeare's collected works, published in 1632. In commendatory verses prefacing an edition of Shakespeare's *Poems* which appeared in 1640, the poet Leonard Digges writes,

> ... let but Beatrice
> And Benedick be seen, lo in a trice
> The Cockpit, galleries, boxes, all are full.

(sig. A4^r)

Digges is referring to the popularity of *Much Ado About Nothing* after Shakespeare's death. The Cockpit was an upmarket indoor theatre in seventeenth-century London.

Once again, the names of the two star protagonists suffice to trigger recognition of the play. In 1862 the comic opera that Hector Berlioz derived from the play was called *Beatrice and Benedick*. The relationship between the lovers inspired the comedy of manners, a genre that was immensely successful during the Restoration period and featured witty dialogue and wordplay amongst fashionable men and women in a high-society setting.

Despite their vivacity and the central role they play in the social life around them, at their core, both characters are outsiders, mavericks who are too unconventional to blindly obey the rules of society. Their exchange of remarks during the masque scene about the communal dance they are apparently a part of is significant. 'We must follow the leaders', Beatrice nudges Benedick, who qualifies her statement with the cryptic comment, 'In every good thing.' Beatrice assents wholeheartedly, adding, 'Nay, if they lead to any ill I will leave them at the next turning' (2.1.137–40). They are only too willing to deviate from the usual path if they do not agree with where it is leading. There is in fact something radically lonely about Beatrice and Benedick. For Barbara Everett, there are affinities between the two characters and the wise fools in later plays by Shakespeare ('The Unsociable Comedy'). In one of the touches of brilliance in the dialogue, Beatrice expresses the loneliness and resilience of both characters poignantly. Don Pedro, admiring her wit, remarks, 'out o'question, you were born in a merry hour'. Beatrice responds, 'No, sure, my lord, my mother cried; but then there was a star danced, and under that was I born' (2.1.306–9). For both Beatrice and Benedick, facing the world with laughter is a conscious strategy to defy pain, not the result of intrinsic cheerfulness.

The humorous banter that is exchanged between the two protagonists does not fail to amuse and entertain contemporary audiences. The erotic spark that is ignited between them still works its magic in performances today. Take, for instance, a typical excerpt from their conversation:

BENEDICK

… And I pray thee now tell me, for which of my bad
parts didst thou first fall in love with me?

BEATRICE

For them all together, which maintain so politic a
state of evil that they will not admit any good parts to
intermingle with them. For which of my good parts did
you first suffer love for me?

BENEDICK

Suffer love – a good epithet. I do suffer love indeed, for
I love thee against my will.

BEATRICE

In spite of your heart, I think. Alas, poor heart. If you
spite it for my sake I will spite it for yours, for I will
never love that which my friend hates.

BENEDICK

Thou and I are too wise to woo peacably.

(5.2.56–67)

In characteristic fashion, Beatrice and Benedick refuse to
respond to romantic cues and turn potentially saccharine
sentiments on their head. Their playful raillery provides a foil
against which we can judge the stilted, artificial relationship
between Claudio and Hero. Their mutual teasing rejects
sentimental pieties and articulates a shared cynical attitude
towards romantic fantasies. Both Beatrice and Benedick are
conscious of their intellectual superiority to all other members
of Messina society. As Benedick puts it paradoxically, they
are both too clever to indulge in the conventional turtledove
demeanour that their society expects of them. Even their
mutual declaration of love is made in a wry, self-mocking tone.

BENEDICK

I do love nothing in the world so well as you. Is not
that strange?

BEATRICE

As strange as the thing I know not. It were as possible

for me to say I loved nothing so well as you. But
believe me not – and yet I lie not. I confess nothing,
nor I deny nothing.

(4.1.267–72)

Although both characters are capable of delivering set pieces
of flamboyant prose, their admission that they, too, have
fallen victim to the malady of love is made in a sponta-
neous, naturalistic idiom. The term they both use repeatedly,
'nothing', conveys their determination to avoid effusive
emotional display and rhetorical appeals to pathos. This
scoffing scepticism is in fact articulated in the title of the
play itself, which is built around a multiple pun. One of the
meanings it conveys is an amused contempt for romance – the
play, it declares, it about nothing very important. It deflates
the fuss that the characters stir up about affairs of the heart.

Puns

The punning title of the play encapsulates its main strands
in a nutshell. Apart from gesturing towards the triviality of
the subject matter, the term 'nothing' carries two further
connotations. 'Nothing' was a bawdy expression for the
female sexual organs. Suggestive puns about 'nothing' are
legion in early modern plays, perhaps most famously in
Hamlet's exchange with Ophelia while watching the play
put on by the travelling players. Hamlet is viciously intent
on humiliating Ophelia for what he seems to regard as her
betrayal of him.

HAMLET
   Lady, shall I lie in your lap?
OPHELIA
   No, my lord.
HAMLET
   Do you think I meant country matters?

OPHELIA
I think nothing, my lord.
HAMLET
That's a fair thought to lie between maids' legs.
OPHELIA
What is, my lord?
HAMLET
Nothing.

(3.2.108–14)

As in the allusion to 'country matters', the term 'nothing', referring to a female lack, would be clear to the audience both in the playhouse and on stage. Apart from the title, *Much Ado About Nothing* makes no explicit mileage out of the ribald pun, but the play is honeycombed with enough salacious jests to draw attention to the off-colour connotations of the word. The protagonists of the main plot are obsessively concerned with the sexual purity or otherwise of Hero. As the title of the play declares, it is centred on female sexuality and the cult of male honour bound up with it.

The third significance of the title is one that takes a little effort to recuperate, but one that immediately becomes clear once we bridge the historical distance between contemporary spoken language and Shakespeare's English. Linguistic experts David and Ben Crystal have done pioneering work in recovering the original pronunciation of words in Shakespeare. They confirm what earlier scholars such as Helge Kökeritz have long proclaimed: the words 'nothing' and 'noting' were pronounced in a very similar manner, which is close to the way we say 'noting' today. The title of *Much Ado About Nothing* gestures towards the incessant activity of surveillance that suffuses the play. Characters are ceaselessly involved in watching each other, noting and studying the behaviour, style, and words of their peers. Eavesdropping on other people appears to be a Messina pastime. The people of the play are fond of wearing masks, but eager to uncover the reality that underlies the performances of others. Much in the same way as the motif of fashion that forms a thread weaving through the play, the language of *Much Ado About Nothing* is pervaded with references to observation.

In Act 1 Scene 1, when Claudio is alone with Benedick on stage, he turns to his companion and asks, 'didst thou note the daughter of Signor Leonato?' Benedick's answer is riddling. 'I noted her not, but I looked on her', he remarks (1.1.154–6). Claudio, by contrast, is deeply engaged in observing Hero carefully. He is only too keen to take advantage of Don John's offer to witness her infidelity in action. His imagined stroke of genius is his masterly interpretation of her facial expressions during the wedding scene.

However, before the main plot unfolds, something strange happens. In two scenes following closely on the heels of the other, characters relate how they have overheard certain crucial conversations. In Act 1 Scene 2, Leonato's brother Antonio discloses some sensational news that he has acquired at second hand.

> The prince and Count Claudio, walking in a thick-pleached alley in mine orchard, were thus much overheard by a man of mine: the prince discovered to Claudio that he loved my niece your daughter, and meant to acknowledge it this night in a dance; and if he found her accordant, he meant to take the present time by the top and instantly break with you of it.
>
> (1.2.7–14)

Leonato is initially sceptical and queries whether the source be reliable, which Antonio hastens to assure him is the case. The audience, on the other hand, have just heard Don Pedro offer to woo Hero as a surrogate for his close associate Claudio. Why either deem this to be necessary remains unexplained, but before the confusion is cleared up, an additional layer is added. In the very next scene, Don John's man Borachio narrates another tale of eavesdropping. Pressed into service to assist in the preparations for festivities by burning aromatic herbs in a disused room, he overhears an exchange between Claudio and Don Pedro.

> Being entertained for a perfumer, as I was smoking a musty room comes me the prince and Claudio, hand in hand in sad conference. I whipped me behind the arras, and there heard it agreed upon that the prince should woo Hero for himself, and having obtained her, give her to Count Claudio.
>
> (1.3.54–9)

Borachio's version comes close to what we earlier heard Don Pedro suggest to Claudio. However, it differs in one respect: the Prince had spoken of courting Hero disguised as Claudio, not as himself: 'I will assume thy part in some disguise / And tell fair Hero I am Claudio' (1.1.302–3). But in the following masque, complications proliferate, and the plot seems to spiral out of control. The scene is punctured with fragments of flirtation between shifting pairs of characters, including Hero and Don Pedro – for a brief moment Hero seems transformed, as if the masks donned by the revellers permit her to slip out of her demure skin and take on the attributes of her cousin. Beatrice meanwhile is deep in conversation with Benedick, whom she ribs unmercifully, apparently in revenge for his deriding her wit. Whether or not she can see through his disguise remains unclear. Don John enters and confides to his accomplice, Borachio, 'Surely my brother is amorous on Hero and hath withdrawn her father to break with him about it' (2.1.141–2). He seems to have changed his mind about his brother's intentions. Before we can draw a breath, both men approach Claudio, pretending to take him for Benedick. Claudio plays along with what he takes for a misconception, for his part assuming the role of his companion. He then receives a torrent of vicious gossip about the Prince and Hero poured into his ear by the villains of the play, which he has no hesitation in believing. But other characters seem to have succumbed to the very same illusion about the Prince's betrayal of his follower and friend. Benedick enters and announces, 'the prince hath got your Hero' (176), and in not exactly the most tactful manner proceeds to enquire, 'But did you think the prince would have served you thus?' (179–80). It is only when the Prince himself speaks to Benedick and disabuses him of the impression that he has wooed Hero for himself that he is persuaded otherwise.

Why, one wonders, does Shakespeare go to such lengths to produce a medley of mystifying impressions in the first two acts, when they have so little to do with the intrigue that forms the climactic part of the plot? Even though the audience has actually witnessed the Prince broach his plan to Claudio, one that he seems to carry out to the letter, doubts begin to mushroom. Who exactly is wooing whom? Apart from Claudio, why do even Don John and Benedick seem to believe that the Prince is involved in a devious plot to gain Hero for himself? Our bewilderment at the very suggestion of courting a woman in place of another man remains unresolved. And what does Hero think of all this? After the initial piece of misinformation, her father will have warned her to be prepared for a proposal of marriage by the Prince himself. Is it all the same to her whether one lover is exchanged for another?

The questions are never answered, and we need to beware of treating dramatic personae as if they were living human beings, even if Shakespeare is a master in creating the impression of real people by adding a few revealing details. What is perhaps of greater interest is the atmosphere conjured up by this string of misapprehensions in the initial scenes. The playworld presented to us is one peopled by characters who are addicted to rumour, calumny and hearsay, and whose first impulse is to dive behind trees or wall hangings and attempt to overhear conversations not intended for their ears. This holds true not just for the sidekicks of the villain, but for all the members of this backwater of intrigue and insinuation. Claudio pretends he is Benedick, and is ironically rewarded with more malicious talk than he could have wished for. Benedick and Beatrice are eager to hear what their friends are saying about them, and fall into the trap of eavesdropping on discussions stage-managed for their consumption. Don Pedro and Claudio spy on Hero, and do not realize how they are being manipulated to see what they are supposed to see. The men of the watch snoop on the villains, and, despite misunderstanding what they hear, stumble on to the truth. And the Friar remains quiet during Claudio's slander of Hero in the wedding scene because he is too busy scrutinizing her: 'I have only been silent so long, / And given way unto this course of fortune, / By noting of the lady', he excuses himself (4.1.156–8), before imparting the wisdom he has garnered through observation. In keeping with the tenor of the play, the solution he proposes is yet another arranged performance: 'a mourning ostentation' (205), a formal show of grieving at a death that has not taken place. Before the main plot gets underway, we are introduced into a world where deception is rife and characters are only too ready to accept tales of betrayal and other stories about those closest to them. Take, for example, a dialogue that we actually witness – the discussion between Don Pedro and Claudio about how to win Hero. It generates a vortex of misprision and sharpens our awareness of the characters' vulnerability to delusions manufactured expressly to trick them.

The effect of the pun on 'noting' is further enhanced by means of a little drama that is played out before the gulling of Benedick commences. Don Pedro and his companions enter the orchard on the pretext of listening to a young musician, Balthasar. The dialogue bears citing in full.

DON PEDRO
    Come, Balthasar, we'll hear that song again.
BALTHASAR
    O good my lord, tax not so bad a voice
    To slander music any more than once.
DON PEDRO
    It is the witness still of excellency
    To put a strange face on his own perfections.
    I pray thee sing, and let me woo no more.

BALTHASAR
    Because you talk of wooing I will sing,
    Since many a wooer doth commence his suit
    To her he thinks not worthy, yet he woos,
    Yet will he swear he loves.
DON PEDRO   Nay, pray thee, come,
    Or if thou wilt hold longer argument,
    Do it in notes.
BALTHASAR   Not this before my notes;
    There's not a note of mine that's worth the noting.
DON PEDRO
    Why, these are very crotchets that he speaks.
    Note notes forsooth, and nothing!
                                            (2.3.41–55)

A further tier of meaning is added to the pun on 'noting',
drawing on the field of music. Don Pedro extends the joke
by introducing a second pun, this time on the word 'crochet',
which could signify either a musical note or a whimsical
fancy, and playfully accuses Balthasar of being coy about his
musical skills in order to elicit further compliments. The entire
exchange epitomizes the culture of courtesy that forms the
backdrop to the play.

Balthasar, who has already performed for the Prince and
his inner circle, who will perform again, and who wins an
assignment to perform the following night as part of the
wooing rituals directed at Hero, demurs at the request to
sing, denigrating his talent with elaborate modesty. What
he presents is, in fact, the strategy of *sprezzatura* outlined
by Castiglione in *The Book of the Courtier* – the display of
elegant nonchalance about one's own abilities. The Prince
detects the move unerringly and immediately turns it into
an exquisite compliment, claiming that it is Balthasar's
diffidence that is the proof of the quality of his art: 'It is
the witness still of excellency / To put a strange face on his
own perfection' (44–5). He continues to entreat Balthasar
to make music, speaking in terms of a lover pursuing a

lady with expressions of endearment. Balthasar picks up the reference and in mock-flirtatious manner points out that many lovers cover their indifference or disdain for the ladies they woo with an impeccable demonstration of love. The quibbling between Don Pedro and the musician continues for a few moments, before Balthasar settles down to sing. Needless to say, the little show is a polished social performance in which the actual relations of power are tastefully concealed. Balthasar, an attendant of the Prince, is not really free to decline the request. It is not quite clear what his status is, but it is probable that he belongs to the fringes of a court society where Claudio and Benedick form the inner circle. Like the messenger whose refined conversation opened the play, Balthasar is a generic minor courtier who seems overeager to imitate the stylish manners of the upper echelons of society, precisely because so much is at stake for him in doing so. In his punning reference to 'noting', he evokes a world in which spying on others and self-surveillance are the norm, and misleading masks, vicious gossip and slander the obverse of the charming manners and elegant exterior of courtly life. Significantly, in his graceful jesting with the Prince, Balthasar speaks metaphorically of 'slandering' music by his bad singing, perhaps personifying music in a reference to the Muses, the classical goddesses thought to nurture the arts.

The song he then proceeds to sing speaks of men as a sex that have swindled and betrayed their lovers since time immemorial: 'Men were deceivers ever' (61). In the brief conversation with his patron, Balthasar talks about men lying to the women they pretend to be in love with. By contrast, the play examines an ideology in which it is women who are inexorably associated with deception, and who invariably betray their lovers. There is no doubt in Claudio's mind first that Hero has seduced the Prince and then that she has been disloyal to him. This ingrained belief in the corruption of women is shared by Don Pedro and even by Leonato, who doubts his own daughter's honesty rather than the accusations of the Prince and his consorts. It is a conviction that forms the foundation for what the critic Harry Berger, Jr, has called 'the Men's Club of Messina' (2001: 21). In the Renaissance, it was subtended by the ideas of aristocratic honour and its converse, shame. This provides one of the main themes of *Much Ado About Nothing*.

Honour and dishonour

Historians such as Keith Thomas and Mervyn James have discussed the distinctive features of the Renaissance concept of honour. A notable change of emphasis took place between the medieval period and the early modern era. The nobility in the Middle Ages were under the sway of the chivalric movement, in which the feudal notion of military honour played an important role. With the emergence of the nation state in the Renaissance, the aristocracy throughout Europe largely lost its martial function. New technological developments in warfare such as gunpowder made man-to-man combat obsolete, while the process of state formation meant that local aristocratic power bases were increasingly attenuated by a centralized polity dominated, to a greater or lesser degree, by an absolutist ruler (Elias 1994 [1939]). Violence was progressively monopolized by the state, and there were fewer and fewer flamboyant outbreaks of aggression by local magnates. The aristocracy were under pressure to redefine themselves and find new sources of legitimation for their role as political and social elite. One of the concepts that evolved in a new direction in this period was the cult of honour.

The term honour had two main meanings. It referred to the esteem accorded to members of the social elite, both by their inferiors and their peer group. At the same time, it related to the outstanding qualities on which this respect was allegedly grounded. The nobility were thought to possess innate qualities that justified their position at the apex of society. During the Renaissance, the Christian ideals that had formed the basis of the ethos of chivalry were gradually displaced by ideas from antiquity (Watson 1976). The classical notion of glory came to take on a central role in the definition of nobility. The Humanists' insistence on education, and their deep interest in the thought of philosophers such as Aristotle and Cicero, led them to initiate what historians such as Quentin Skinner have seen as a deeply political and potentially radical project: the idea that the right to rule was based not on birth, but virtue. As Humanist thinkers stressed, in his *Politics* (1932) Aristotle had defined aristocracy on the basis of merit and wealth, not lineage. Honour, he had made clear in the *Nicomachean Ethics* (2009), was the reward accorded to those of outstanding virtue. The ability to govern was now defined as being grounded on education and personal virtue.

Perhaps it might be helpful at this point to clarify what the ancients meant by virtue. The main sources that early moderns drew upon in this connection were Aristotle's *Nicomachean Ethics* and Cicero's *De Officiis* [*On Obligations*] (2000), works that were enormously influential in this period. Both thinkers described a bundle of qualities, chief amongst them wisdom, justice, fortitude and temperance. These qualities were regarded as typical characteristics of the governing members of society. A crucial virtue was magnanimity (often termed 'greatness of soul'). Magnanimity implied a sense of pride and a lofty bearing, which was expressed in disregard for danger and profit – meanness and pettiness – and entailed a courteous demeanour towards those of simple origin. A gentleman revealed his qualities, above all his magnanimity, not only in the way he behaved, but also in the way he moved, the way he spoke, and the way he looked. His inner virtue was expressed in his outward appearance and his manners.

In reality, nobility was predominantly a matter of wealth displayed in an appropriate lifestyle. In an age that according to some historians saw the birth of a consumer society (Thirsk 1978), conspicuous consumption of commodities, clothes,

fashion, hospitality, servants and housing was a badge of
gentility. Courtesy books spell out the need to display one's
status in fitting manner. Renaissance theorists admitted that
virtue was what justified the right of the ruling class to govern,
but tended to argue that it was the nobility that happened to
be the most abundantly endowed with it. Stephano Guazzo in
his *Civile Conversation* puts it succinctly: 'Absolute gentlemen
are those who to their gentrie by birth and vertue have great
riches joined, which serve greatly to the maintenance of
gentrie' (1586 [1581], 1.186). The assumption that what
distinguished members of the aristocracy from lesser mortals
was their inner rectitude or sense of honour needed to be
constantly reasserted. The corollary of honour, the desire
to avoid shame, functioned as a form of social discipline
reinforcing received norms. A loss of reputation had devastating consequences, both for men and women. Dishonour
meant losing face and earning the contempt of one's peers.
The greatest insult that could be hurled at an opponent was
to accuse him of lying: 'giving someone the lie'. A nobleman
was marked off from the rest of humanity by his integrity and
trustworthiness. Keeping one's word was an integral part of a
gentleman's ethos.

Accusing a gentleman of lying inevitably resulted in a
challenge, but only to someone from the rank of gentry
or above. Paradoxically, the duel of honour was a feature
of the Renaissance ideology of courtesy and a product of
the court culture of early modern Italy (Peltonen 2003). A
notion of personal honour took over from the feuds carried
out between aristocratic families or factions. Since they led
to a decline in large-scale violence, duels were defended as
contributing to an increase in civility. Duelling was not, as
one might think, a remnant of feudal rites. Instead, it was
very much a Renaissance phenomenon, and reflects the rise of
individualism in the early modern era. The Italian fashion for
private duels took hold of the whole of Europe. The duel was
linked to the change in weaponry that was associated with the
aristocracy – the heavy sword of the Middle Ages was replaced

by the light rapier, ideal for thrusting. In England, in the late sixteenth century, Italian masters such as Vincentio Saviolo opened fashionable fencing schools and even published a manual of the rules that governed correct duelling. The court fool Touchstone mocks the vogue for duels in *As You Like It*, scoffing, 'we quarrel in print, by the book, as you have books for good manners' (5.4.89–90).

Much Ado About Nothing is a play imbued with ideas of honour and the Renaissance culture of courtesy in which they are entrenched. At the beginning of the play the aristocratic characters have just returned from wars, yet military honour plays only a minor part in their self-definition. Instead, their sense of distinction is displayed in their graceful manners, their preoccupation with a stylish exterior and their witty discourse. They accord respect to their peers in mutual courtesies, a polished veneer that conceals the realities of power, competition for the favour of the prince, and the incessant spying and idle talk that underlie these realities. The metaphor of fashion that traverses the play suggests a society absorbed with style and appearances as well as one in the grip of social norms about how to behave. The clowns of the play ape their betters in their fascination with modish language – and in their gullibility for surface appearances. One powerful instrument to make a rival lose face was to accuse the women with whom they were associated of sexual disloyalty. Notions of chastity formed an important tool with which to enforce social discipline. The motif of sexual honour runs through the play, from the cuckoldry jokes and the bastardy of Don John to the plot against Hero and Claudio's decision to shame her in public.

Shame

For women of all classes, the most devastating dishonour was to be accused of a lack of chastity. Once lost, their honour could almost never be recovered. The death that Hero feigns in *Much Ado About Nothing* is an apt metaphor for the social death that the slander perpetrated against her would have meant in real life. In early modern England, slander and defamation were of vital importance to the reputation of a woman. The vast majority of slander suits involving women centred on accusations of sexual impropriety. The good name of a woman was bound up with the honour of the men she was subordinate to, be it her father or her husband (Cerasano 2001). Accordingly, when Claudio is confronted with the falsehood planted by Don John about Hero's infidelity, he insists on disassociating himself from her in a highly public manner.

It is in the church scene that the calamitous dimensions of the accusation become apparent. The violence of the rhetoric deployed by Claudio, Don Pedro and Leonato is palpable. Claudio rejects his bride as a 'rotten orange' and announces that her honour is mere facade: 'She's but the sign and semblance of her honour' (4.1.30–1). Hero is then dissected as an exemplar of the grossest sexual depravity. Claudio elaborates,

> You seem to me as Dian in her orb,
> As chaste as is the bud ere it be blown;
> But you are more intemperate in your blood
> Than Venus, or those pampered animals
> That rage in savage sensuality.
>
> (56–60)

He compares Hero's appearance to that of Diana, the goddess of chastity, and the bud of a blossom, a conventional image for sexual innocence. Yet in reality, he claims, Hero is as lustful as Venus, goddess of love. Without a pause, his imagery then thrusts her even lower, to the level of lascivious beasts, governed solely by passion.

The dishonour is not one that affects Claudio alone. The Prince is contaminated as the result of his involvement in the engagement: 'I stand dishonoured that have gone about / To link my dear friend to a common stale' (63–4), he declares, explicitly labelling Hero as a 'stale', or prostitute. It is also clear that Claudio wishes to implicate Leonato, his prospective father-in-law, in the degradation of Hero. Hero has been the object of exchange in an intended alliance between Claudio and Leonato. For the latter, the prestige of marrying his daughter to someone of Claudio's status would have been ample recompense for bestowing his fortune on the young man. Now that Hero turns out to be shop-soiled, Claudio is keen to humiliate her father. When the Friar formally enquires of the bridegroom whether he knows of any impediment to the marriage, Leonato genially throws in, 'I dare make his answer: none.' Claudio turns on the older man with a sneer: 'O, what men dare do! What men may do! What men daily do, not knowing what they do!' (16–18). Ordering the Friar to stand aside, he then proceeds to act out a little travesty of the betrothal ceremony. The entire playlet of acceptance and rejection is aimed at shaming Leonato and making him lose face in front of the large congregation of his peers that he has invited to his daughter's wedding. Claudio makes it evident that he aligns himself with the Prince, who represents true nobility, as opposed to the aspiring gentry that Leonato stands for. The insulting behaviour of Claudio and Don Pedro has the required effect. There might have been many ways of responding to the public disgracing of one's only daughter. Leonato's reaction is first to contemplate killing himself for shame: 'Hath no man's dagger a point for me?' (109). He yearns for death to release him from his dishonour. But it is his daughter who collapses and appears to have died of shock. Leonato welcomes what seems to be her death, and comments, 'Death is the fairest cover for her shame / That may be wished for' (116–17). He then turns to viciously attack his child, exclaiming, 'doth not every earthly thing / Cry shame upon her?' (120–21). Seeing that Hero seems to be rallying, he urges her to die.

Do not live, Hero; do not ope thine eyes!
For did I think thou wouldst not quickly die,

Thought I thy spirits were stronger than thy shames,
Myself would on the rearward of reproaches
Strike at thy life.

(123–7)

He threatens that, if his daughter does not die of shame, he
will take charge of killing her himself. The words he uses to
revile her offers a revealing insight into Shakespeare's use of
language for the purpose of characterization. With a few deft
strokes, Leonato's personality stands dissected to the audience.

Grieved I, I had but one?
Chid I for that at frugal Nature's frame?
O, one too much by thee! Why had I one?
Why ever wast thou lovely in my eyes?
Why had I not with charitable hand
Took up a beggar's issue at my gates,
Who smirched thus, and mired with infamy,
I might have said: 'No part of it is mine;
This shame derives itself from unknown loins.'
But mine, and mine I loved, and mine I praise,
And mine that I was proud on – mine so much
That I myself was to myself not mine
Valuing of her. Why she – O, she is fallen
Into a pit of ink that the wide sea
Hath drops too few to wash her clean again,
And salt too little which may season give
To her foul-tainted flesh.

(127–43)

Leonato's pain seems genuine and is deeply compelling.
However, as his string of rhetorical questions reveal, his grief
circulates entirely around himself. Personal and possessive
pronouns are piled on so relentlessly that the effect of
boundless solipsism is inescapable. Leonato reproaches
himself for ever having mourned his lack of other children.
In a grotesque flight of fancy, he castigates himself for not

having adopted a beggar child, instead of fathering Hero. If the adopted foundling had dishonoured his name in the way his own daughter has done, he could have disowned her, and might have remained untouched by shame. He assails Hero for her ingratitude for the love lavished on her, and uses hyberbolical imagery of extraordinary filth and contamination to describe her situation – her reputation is so blackened that the water of the entire ocean would not suffice to remove the taint of her guilt; her flesh is so polluted that all the salt in the sea would not be able to cover the rankness. The metaphors of putrifying flesh and indelible stains are ones that Shakespeare will re-use in a number of tragedies such as *Hamlet*, *Othello* and *Macbeth*, but that are quite startling in the context of a comedy.

Leonato's self-centredness is one element in Shakespeare's project of excoriating the cult of honour, but it needs to be set in the context of his time. Leonato is in thrall to the notion that noblemen, particularly those of the highest rank, cannot be wrong. 'Would the two princes lie, and Claudio lie / Who loved her so, that speaking of her foulness / Washed it with tears?', he asks rhetorically, according Claudio the complimentary rank of a person of royal blood (152–4). The audience has seen no token of Claudio's grief, only signs of endless smugness, but Leonato is convinced that the aristocratic suitor of his daughter cannot have been at fault. Once doubt has seeped into his mind, however, he responds in the only way possible within the ideology of honour – by issuing a challenge to the two noblemen: 'if they wrong her honour, / The proudest of them shall well hear of it' (191–2). Indeed, when Leonato and his brother Antonio next encounter the Prince and Claudio, a farcical scenario ensues in which the two old men unsuccessfully attempt to compel the young aristocrats to fight a duel. The scene evokes a mixture of hilarity and pathos, and we watch the Prince and Claudio brush off their attacks with casual contempt. Far more uncomfortable is the thought that, as some critics argue, not only the older generation of men but young women such as Hero and Beatrice are complicit in the ideology of honour.

In the grand strategy of Don Pedro to make Benedick and Beatrice fall in love with each other, Hero's allotted part is to convince Beatrice that Benedick is smitten by love for her. As we have seen, she departs from her role, and focuses her attention on shaming her cousin. To Ursula she remarks of Beatrice 'she is too disdainful', adding a simile taken from the field of falconry: 'her spirits are as coy and wild / As haggards of the rock' (3.1.34–6). Haggards are wild female hawks whom falconers capture and train for the purposes of hunting. Beatrice's temperament is anything but 'coy'; what Hero is referring to is her reluctance to surrender to the bond of marriage and the curtailing of her liberty that it would lead to. Early modern gender norms were built on the notion that women were subordinate to men – to their fathers and brothers before they were married, and to their husbands after entering the state of marriage. Beatrice, who seems to be an orphan living in the household of her uncle, Leonato, who treats her with affection and enjoys her spirited discourse, lives a life of relative freedom, particularly as regards her unbridled tongue. Hero seems to believe that, like a hawk, Beatrice's spirit should be broken, and she should be taught to obey. As she puts it censoriously, 'to be so odd and from all fashions / As Beatrice is cannot be commendable' (72–3). Beatrice, Hero claims, needs to learn to abandon her pursuit of independence and embrace the role of women dictated by early modern gender paradigms, once more using the term 'fashion' to refer to social discipline. She chastises her cousin for her disdain, suggesting that her pride needs to be humbled. For Harry Berger, Jr, the 'implied contrast is, of course, with her own quiet, reliable, unappreciated girl-scout self' (2001: 18). Berger detects a combination of resentment and grudging admiration for her cousin as the main motives underlying Hero's words. By humiliating Beatrice, Hero attempts to bring her down to her own level, and to force her to accept a submissive role as a woman's lot in life. It is to this end that she announces, 'I'll devise some honest slanders / To stain my cousin with' (84–5). Her unwittingly ironic use of this expression reveals how deeply her thought is embedded in the cult of honour. 'Honest' was a term rooted in 'honour', a meaning it has largely lost today. Hero's words are reinforced by two layers of oxmoronic meaning, yoking together the opposing ideas of truth and lies and those of honour and dishonour.

Hero herself becomes the victim of a cruel shaming ritual, grounded on the notion that a woman's honour was defined through her chastity. At the end of the play, once the truth has come to light, the Friar and her father devise another series of rituals to redeem her reputation and restore her marriage. Claudio and the Prince are condemned to undergo a purification by mourning, even though the tomb at which they mourn is empty. Next, a second betrothal takes place, with a masked Hero put forward as a fictive cousin. Only once they have been united in wedlock does Hero lift her veil.

HERO
   [*Unmasks*] And when I lived I was your other wife;
   And when you loved, you were my other husband.
CLAUDIO
   Another Hero!
HERO   Nothing certainer.
   One Hero died defiled, but I do live,
   And surely as I live, I am a maid.

                              (5.4.60–4)

The plan devised by Leonato and the Friar is aimed at effecting a transformation in Claudio and the Prince. Her lines are ambiguous, but it seems as if Hero herself has undergone a change. She distances herself from her previous life and from the slander that destroyed her reputation. For the critic Susan Cerasano, with these words she takes control of language to create her own reality (2001: 48). Perhaps she no longer defines herself solely in relation to sexual honour. The term

'maid', which meant both 'virgin' and simply 'young woman'
(*OED* 1a and 2a), could refer both to her chastity and to her
dignity as a human being.

For Beatrice, the issue of honour is less a question of shaming
other women than a matter of revenge. She calls on Benedick
to challenge his companion, Claudio, to exact retribution for
dishonouring her relative. Shrewdly, she discerns how deliberately Claudio and Don Pedro have planned the public disgrace
of Hero. 'What, bear her in hand until they come to take hands,
and then with public accusation, uncovered slander, unmitigated
rancour?' (4.1.302–4) As she notes, the entire performance has
been a calculated and malicious attempt to harm Hero in the
most effective way, with a carefully orchestrated sequence
of steps leading to the cataclysmic moment of denunciation.
She counters the vicious rhetoric used by the Prince and the
Count with violent language of her own: 'I would eat his heart
in the marketplace' (305). In fact, the words she utters, 'Kill
Claudio' (288), have a similarly jarring impact as the insult
Claudio hurled at Leonato earlier in the same scene: 'Give
not this rotten orange to your friend' (30). Both are spoken
in a context where they are utterly unexpected – in the case of
Claudio, a wedding ceremony, and in the case of Beatrice, the
point at which the reluctant pair of lovers finally admit their
feelings for each other. The audience has been eagerly awaiting
this moment, and the explosive words are a jolting reminder of
the darker side of the play. Beatrice, who throughout the play
has rejected the role of compliant femininity that early modern
culture holds out for her, and whose fantasies are of mingling
with men and women on a basis of equality, repeatedly wishes
that she were a man and were able to challenge Claudio to a
duel. She passionately denounces the culture of civility that she
considers has turned men into mincing paragons of fashion –
into a mere façade of manliness.

> Princes and counties! Surely a princely testimony, a goodly
> count! Count Comfit, a sweet gallant surely. O that I were a
> man for his sake! Or that I had any friend would be a man

for my sake! But manhood is melted into curtsies, valour
into compliment, and men are only turned into tongue, and
trim ones, too. He is now as valiant as Hercules that only
tells a lie and swears it. I cannot be a man with wishing,
therefore I will die a woman with grieving.

(4.1.313–21)

Beatrice's fury lends her powers of expression added brilliance,
and she spits out a string of puns, all mocking Claudio. She
sarcastically calls him 'a goodly count', referring to his title as
well as to what she considers his tall tale or account, and also,
in a play on the legal meaning of 'count', to his accusation.
His cloying mannerisms as lover earn him the epithet 'Count
Comfit' – comfit was an Elizabethan word for a sweet. Her
outburst against Claudio runs on to include all men, whom
she indicts in a series of parallel clauses freighted with alliterative antonyms, opposing the words 'manhood', 'valour'
and 'men' to 'curtsies', 'compliment' and 'tongue', which she
qualifies with yet another alliteration, the adjective 'trim'.
The cluster of terms she lists contrast true manliness with
fashionable manners and elegant speech. Men are no longer
defined through courage, but through lying, which by association she links to courteous speech. She adduces the classical
hero Hercules to underscore her point, once more mourning
the lack of real men in the world, and regretting the fact that,
as a woman, she is not able to take decisive action. The set of
balanced clauses in which she articulates her lament, in which
she sets off a man against a woman and desire against sorrow,
only help her make her case more powerfully.

Curiously, the figure of Hercules haunts *Much Ado About
Nothing* – Beatrice's diatribe contains the fourth mention of
the hero in the play. Three of the four references allude to the
myth of Hercules during his period of servitude to the Oriental
queen Omphale, and contain mocking remarks about his lack
of masculinity. In addition, there is a fifth, indirect reference
to the Greek hero. The first citation of Hercules is by Benedick
who, when complaining about Beatrice to the Prince, claims

she would have outdone Omphale in unmanning Hercules: 'She would have made Hercules have turned spit, yea, and cleft his club to make the fire too' (2.1.231–3). In the legend, Omphale dressed Hercules in women's clothes and set him the task of helping the womenfolk with their weaving, but Benedick has Beatrice give Hercules an even more demeaning role to fulfil – helping out in the kitchen. Hercules' massive club was symbolic of his strength; Beatrice, Benedick declared at the time, would have made him destroy his own club to stoke the kitchen fires. The emasculating connotations of his hilarious riff on the Greek hero are patent. Admittedly, this harangue about Beatrice was provoked by her taunting him at the masque and injuring his sense of pride by insinuating that his status is no higher than that of a professional entertainer at court. It is part and parcel of his chorus of denials that he will ever marry.

As for the other two explicit references to Hercules, one occurs in the broadside against fashion delivered by Borachio, discussed in Chapter 2. Fashion, the drunken villain declares, turns men into dupes, and he draws an analogy to 'the shaven Hercules in the smirched worm-eaten tapestry, where his codpiece seems as massy as his club' (3.3.131–3). Hercules might appear to be well endowed in old wall hangings, but the fact that he has no beard reveals how effeminate he has become. There is an additional, implicit reference to Hercules earlier in the play, when Beatrice laughingly rejects the idea of an effeminate husband, saying, 'What should I do with him? Dress him in my apparel and make him my waiting-gentlewoman?' (2.1.29–30).

Lastly, it is Don Pedro who brings up Hercules when he reveals his plot to make Benedick and Beatrice fall in love with each other. This, he declares, would be akin to 'one of Hercules' labours' (2.1.336–7). Don Pedro's idea, however tongue in cheek, of what constitutes a worthwhile endeavour seems to exemplify exactly what Beatrice, one of his victims, is berating – the frivolous pastimes with which the members of Messina high society while away their hours, and their preoccupation with questions of style rather than substance. What Beatrice seems to be unaware of is the fact that the revenge ethos she espouses is only the obverse of the aristocratic cult of honour, in which prestige and reputation are the highest goods (Cook 1995).

Perhaps it is in Benedick's decision to abandon his former companions and take the side of Beatrice that we find the most courageous stance against the dominant code of honour offered by the play. In spite of his former denigration of women, and the high store he seems to set by male camaraderie, Benedick takes the radical step of changing his allegiance and discontinuing his source of employment. He bids farewell to the Prince with the words 'My lord, for your many courtesies, I thank you. I must discontinue your company' (5.1.183–4). To Claudio he issues a challenge to a duel, as Beatrice wished. The reason he gives is, as he puts it, 'In a false quarrel there is no true valour' (120). He might be referring to the falseness of the allegation against Hero – he has taken Beatrice's insistence on the innocence of her cousin on trust, a value that is conspicuously lacking in Claudio's relationship to his own fiancée. Or he might be making a larger point – that a notion of male honour as intimately tied up with the chastity of women is inherently flawed. For all the attraction of the glamorous world of stylish people that *Much Ado About Nothing* presents, the play also reveals the hollowness of the culture of honour. It queries the notion of honour put forward by most of the protagonists. In effect, a shift in the definition of honour was gradually taking place in the early modern era. The philosopher Charles Taylor has described how the aristocratic honour ethic is transposed inward into a sense of the dignity of each individual. An aristocratic concept rooted in a hierarchical social structure, honour diminished in importance once human beings were no longer defined predominantly through their social role. To be sure, the respect of our peers remains an important value in our lives. However, our understanding of what this implies is in a continual state of flux. The scholar Kwame Anthony

Appiah has taken a close look at important moral transformations in the history of civilization, such as the abolition of slavery or the decline of footbinding in China. In his book *The Honor Code: How Moral Revolutions Happen* (2010), he argues that changes in codes of honour occur when people are shamed out of an old way of doing something. It seems that in the course of social change a continuous mutation in codes of dishonour becomes discernible. In some societies vindictive rituals of humiliation on the grounds of the importance of sexual honour become increasingly less acceptable. Slander about the alleged sexual misconduct by women is no longer conceded such tremendous power to destroy lives. *Much Ado About Nothing* exposes a world in which a fixation on sexual honour is closely intertwined with an uncritical acceptance of words and surface impressions as the reflection of reality. Perhaps the most probing questions it asks is about the relation of appearances and the truth underlying them.

Appearance and reality

In Chapter 2, we briefly discussed the early modern celebration of the art of rhetoric. For Erasmus, speech was the distinguishing mark of humankind. Early Humanist thinkers had implicit faith in the power of the word – its ability to persuade people to the good, its role in uncovering the truth. What had little place in their thought was the consideration of what it meant if language were to be harnessed for malign purposes, as in slander and calumny. In the course of the early modern age, the initial enthusiasm for rhetoric gave way to an increasing scepticism about language (Ascoli and Kahn 1993). The ambivalent attitude towards rhetoric might have been intensified by the political situation in Italy. A devastating wave of invasions of the peninsula by foreign powers, which began in the late fifteenth century, ended the independence of the flourishing city states. In addition, the Humanist ideal of educating the rulers was felt to have been an overwhelming failure. Disillusionment about the abuse of persuasive language for immoral ends became widespread, and confidence in the close relationship between eloquent speech and inner virtue was more and more eroded. In reality, doubts about rhetoric were not a new development. They hark back to debates that had raged in antiquity between supporters of rhetoric and its detractors. The most famous attack on the ethical basis of rhetoric was made by Plato. His dialogue *Gorgias* was hugely influential and set the parameters for arguments about rhetoric ever since.

Gorgias was an ancient philosopher who specialized in rhetoric. He belonged to a school of thinkers known as Sophists, who were professional teachers who taught the skills of oratory and argumentation to their affluent clients for a fee, a practice that was heavily criticized by Socrates and Aristotle. In dialogue with Socrates, he comes across as a cynical opportunist who is interested in rhetoric as the art of cajoling others, not as a path to gaining insight into truth. Rhetoric was a tool of power that would enable one to convince others to adopt one's own viewpoint. The ethics of what one was arguing was irrelevant. For Socrates, language ought to be used solely to instil virtue into citizens. What Gorgias was describing was not an art, but an artful talent in pleasing people by telling them what they wanted to hear. Famously, Socrates draws an analogy between rhetoric and cooking. With regard to the human body, medicine and gymnastics provide cures and salutary means to improve health – these are what he calls arts. A practice that uses gratification to gain its ends is nothing but flattery.

> It seems to me then, Gorgias, to be a pursuit that is not a matter of art, but showing a shrewd, gallant spirit which has a natural bent for clever dealing with mankind, and I sum up its substance in the name *flattery*. This practice, as I view it, has many branches, and one of them is cookery; which appears indeed to be an art but, by my account of it,

is not an art but a habitude or knack. I call rhetoric another branch of it, as also personal adornment and sophistry – four branches of it for four kinds of affairs.

(463a–b)

It might be helpful to bear in mind that when Plato, who recorded the dialogue – Socrates himself has not left us a single line – is using the term 'art' (*techne*), he is referring to something more akin to a craft than what we might term art. The ancients differentiated between different forms of art: *techne* was the word used for a skill that served a practical purpose, while *poesis* was the term that might generally be said to describe the creation of beauty. What is at stake in the debate between Socrates and Gorgias is the goal any practice aimed for. The end of all action should be the good, not pleasure, Socrates argues. He lumps rhetoric with cookery, sophistry – a debased form of philosophy in Socrates' mind, which failed to strive for the good – and adornment. All four skills might create pleasure, but it was far more important to instruct people how to be virtuous. Instead, what these arts were concerned with was catering to our fondness for superficialities.

Socrates admits that there might be a kind of rhetoric that would be ethically acceptable and that would serve to improve the morals of the people. However, he has never encountered an orator or statesman of Athens who has set his sights on this target. In the coming centuries, Socrates' qualification of his critique of rhetoric rapidly dropped out of the picture. What was continually rehearsed in the controversy between defenders and proponents of rhetoric was the Platonic argument that rhetoric was merely a superficial art that appealed to the senses or catered to the emotions rather than directing our attention to the truth. It pandered to our eternal fascination with surface impressions.

In the early modern period, the criticism of eloquent language was subsumed under a larger attack on pleasing exteriors as opposed to essences. It gained a fresh impetus in the fiery polemic that circulated during the Reformation. Religious reformers insisted that rather than an outward show of religious practice, it was one's inner feeling that counted. They launched a virulent assault on the ceremonies, images and rituals of the Roman Catholic Church, which they branded as idolatrous. Humankind was too busy worshipping external signs to pay proper reverence to God, they claimed. Attractive appearances and ornament only served to distract us from the real truth – the Word of God. They were delusionary phenomena that deceived us about the only reality that mattered. A ferocious drive to eradicate images and pleasing shows of every kind erupted throughout Europe. In England, sacred relics were smashed, religious statues were defaced and medieval decorations were destroyed. The crusade against idolatry touched upon the lives of ordinary citizens, too – in Stratford-upon-Avon, Shakespeare's birthplace, it was Shakespeare's father, town bailiff at the time, who was given the order in 1563 to whitewash the wall paintings in the Guild Chapel. And it was the abolishment of religious drama that led to the spectacular rise of the commercial theatre in London, which made his son immortal.

In the meantime, there were other ways the Renaissance responded to the debate about rhetoric and truth, appearances and reality. Perhaps the most drastic attack on the optimism of early Humanists was made by Machiavelli in his masterpiece *The Prince* (1515). For Cicero, the highest goal for a man was to enhance his honour. The way to achieve this was through virtuous living. As we have seen, Humanists strongly endorsed the Ciceronian emphasis on virtue as indispensable to a member of the ruling class in order to govern well. Machiavelli shares the view that the most important good to aim for was honour and glory, but he differs radically about how to fulfil this aspiration. The core precept, according to Machiavelli, was to adapt to the situation at hand. If this involved immoral acts, so be it. To rule wisely, there was no necessity to be virtuous. The important thing was to maintain the appearance of virtue. What counted was the image, not the reality.

Machiavelli was endlessly vilified for his views and condemned as cynical and unethical. He was widely regarded as the source of the political principles he expounded; his name became a byword for cunning and depravity. A popular stage villain – a 'Machiavel' – emerged, who was a devilish, unscrupulous schemer, and combined elements of the cruel tyrant, a favourite character in tragedies by the Roman playwright Seneca, with the comic devil or his henchman in medieval drama known as the Vice. The 'Machiavel' was a roaring success in the theatre and he inspired a host of figures such as Christopher Marlowe's devious villain Barabas in *The Jew of Malta*, a pair of crafty Venetians, Volpone and Mosca, in Ben Jonson's *Volpone*, and the murderous malcontent Bosola in John Webster's *Duchess of Malfi*. Shakespeare's own Machiavellian characters include his Richard III, Iago in *Othello* and Edmund in *King Lear*. Admittedly, a number of Elizabethans – amongst them Walter Raleigh and Francis Bacon – paid tribute to Machiavelli's acuity in analysing the workings of power and in exposing political realities.

By contrast, Castiglione was the darling of Renaissance society. His description of the importance of presenting an elegant exterior and displaying polish in one's manners, speech and dress was embraced as a guidebook by courtiers all over Europe and formed the template for an entire genre, the Renaissance courtesy book. A significant number of these texts were addressed to social hopefuls in the lower ranks of society. Castiglione's notion of *sprezzatura* (or nonchalance) articulated the imperative of creating the right impression. It was not sufficient to acquire a slew of courtly skills; it was far more effective to produce a facade of effortlessness in all one said and did. Castiglione's courtiers go even further. Count Ludovico Canossa, the chief inter-locutor in Book 1, explains to the select circle that acquiring an air of nonchalance did not merely assist in presenting one's talents in the best possible light. There was a bonus to be had. *Sprezzatura*, brings with it another adornment which, when it accompanies any human action however small, not only reveals at once how much the person knows who does it, but often causes it to be judged much greater than it actually is, since it impresses upon the minds of the onlookers the opinion that he who performs well with so much facility must possess even great skill than this, and that, if he were to devote care and effort to what he does, he could do it far better.

(1.28)

By putting on a front of insouciance one could delude one's peers into thinking that one possessed qualities one did not actually have. In other words, it was a blueprint for deception. The genre Castiglione adopts, the dialogue, enables him to incorporate critique of the ideas put forward in the book within the text itself. Accordingly, one of the courtiers protests emphatically. In Book 2 Gaspare Pallavicino objects, 'This seems to me to be not an art, but an actual deceit.' In response, Federico Fregoso declares, 'This is an ornament attending the thing done, rather than deceit; and even if it be deceit, it is not to be censured.' He goes on to cite the example of a goldsmith who skilfully enhances the beauty of a jewel and claims, 'Surely he deserves praise for that deceit, because with good judgement and art his masterful hand often adds grace and adornment to ivory or to silver or to a beautiful stone by setting it in fine gold' (2.40).

The line Fregoso is treading is a fine one. First, he attempts to whitewash the idea of deceit by replacing the term with 'ornament'. Next, he draws an analogy to a jewel and the skill with which a craftsman sets off the properties of a precious stone. What he evades is the question whether the strategy of *sprezzatura* might be applied to cover a lack instead of to present an accomplishment in a better light. In truth, the response Castiglione offers to the vexed issue of appearance and reality is not very different from that of Machiavelli. For the latter, whether or not the Prince was virtuous was largely irrelevant. Of paramount importance was the semblance of virtue, not what qualities the Prince might actually possess. Similarly, Castiglione's courtiers advocate dissembling if it is useful in creating the impression that the courtier excels in a particular field. The truth is beside the point – all that matters is the appearance.

Seeming and being in *Much Ado About Nothing*

In *Much Ado About Nothing* Shakespeare explores the relationship between appearances and reality from a myriad of perspectives. The play presents a world of glittering surfaces and exquisite social performances in a society that clearly sets great store by style and fashion. The discourse of the characters sparkles with wit and double entendre while the characters are busy playing games of dissimulation with each other. For no clear reason, when wooing Hero for Claudio, Don Pedro pretends he is Claudio; for no clear reason, when approached by Don John and Borachio, Claudio pretends he is Benedick; for no clear reason, Don John pretends to Claudio and his brother that Hero is disloyal. All characters are incessantly involved in spying or eavesdropping on each other. But instead of these activities making for heightened transparency, the play is permeated with examples of misprision. Antonio's servant misunderstands the conversation between Don Pedro and Claudio that he has overheard. Borachio, who overhears the same conversation, reports a version that does not quite tally with what we have witnessed. The members of the watch, snooping on Borachio and Conrade, misapprehend their conversation, and Dogberry misinterprets the misquoted report of their words even further. Dogberry misses the import of the malefactors' confession; Leonato overlooks the significance of the arrest communicated to him on the eve of the wedding. In the meanwhile, Benedick and Beatrice misread each other's behaviour in the light of the false information they have gleaned from their eavesdropping.

As A. P. Rossiter (1967) points out, the masque in Act 2 is an apt symbol of the controlling theme of seeming and being. The protagonists literally slip on masks, and, as in a hall of mirrors, delusions run riot. Claudio mistakenly believes the Prince is betraying him, and Benedick too misjudges the situation. Even Don John is deluded by the sight of his brother courting Hero. Characters claim to be play-acting themselves, as a light-hearted but suggestive fragment of conversation makes clear. Ursula thinks she has seen through Antonio's disguise and asserts, 'I know you well enough; you are Signor Antonio.' Antonio denies that this is the case, and when she insists, reveals, 'To tell you true, I counterfeit him' (2.1.101–5). The joke is on the audience, too: since Antonio will be wearing a mask, we might begin to doubt our own belief in his identity. And in a teasing twist, at a further level the falsehood is expressing the truth: what we see is an actor counterfeiting Antonio who is pretending to be someone else counterfeiting Antonio.

While keen to hoodwink other characters, the citizens of Messina are themselves highly susceptible to the ruses perpetrated on them. When addressed by Don John during the masque, Claudio feigns to be Benedick, but he is nevertheless misled by him into believing the Prince has betrayed him. Before succumbing to his brother's conspiracy, Don Pedro initiates a complicated prank to dupe Benedick and Beatrice, and ropes in all the members of Messina society. Benedick thinks he is prying on the Prince and his companions, while they are the ones engaged in duping him. Similarly, Beatrice believes she is spying on Hero and Ursula, while they are the ones fooling her. Hoaxes proliferate during the last part of the play: the Friar proposes a subterfuge whereby Leonato and his party pretend Hero has died, they stage a mourning ritual at an empty tomb, and the wedding finally takes place with Hero counterfeiting a cousin who does not exist.

Significantly, the ostensible betrayal by Hero that the plot hinges on is a show stage-managed by Don John with no basis in reality. Don John's enigmatic statement to Don Pedro and Claudio, 'If you dare not trust that you see, confess not that you know' (3.2.107–8), posits an intrinsic link between appearances and the truth that is entirely fraudulent. The two gullible noblemen are unaware of the undertones of malice in his remark. As the play mockingly makes clear, they are willing to believe the illusion on mere hearsay before it actually appears before their eyes. Claudio immediately devises a plan how to humiliate his bride to the greatest possible effect, and Don Pedro staunchly declares, 'I will join with thee to disgrace her' (114–15).

It is the church scene that most clearly exposes the ambiguity of appearances and their fraught relation with reality. In his denunciation of Hero, Claudio insists that she is 'but the sign and semblance of her honour' (4.1.31). Hero's honour, which is equated with her chastity, is only a façade, Claudio claims. It is not grounded in reality. He launches into a diatribe against the depravity of his intended bride, paradoxically adducing the fact that she is blushing as evidence.

> Behold how like a maid she blushes here!
> O, what authority and show of truth
> Can cunning sin cover itself withal!
> Comes not that blood as modest evidence
> To witness simple virtue? Would you not swear,
> All you that see her, that she were a maid,
> By these exterior shows? But she is none;
> She knows the heat of a luxurious bed.
> Her blush is guiltiness, not modesty.
>
> (32–40)

Blushing would normally point to the virtue of a woman and serve as a signal of her shamefastness at hearing an accusation of unchastity. But with regard to Hero, her blush is merely a clever guise that she has adopted – she is corrupt to the core. Claudio personifies sin as cleverly cloaking itself with a mantle of truth, but his metaphor merges sin with Hero, attempting to conceal her disgrace beneath the façade of virtue. In reality, he contends, Hero is blushing not from a feeling of modest shame, but from guilt at her history of lascivious acts.

By sleight of hand, Claudio turns what was usually seen as a mark of innocence into an indication of Hero's culpability. There is a radical opposition between her exterior and her inner self, he asserts. But unlike the audience he is addressing, both on stage and in the theatre, Claudio thinks himself too canny to be ensnared by appearances. For his discerning eye, her blush is a visual confession. Claudio continues to harp on the discrepancy between Hero's outward aspect and her inward truth. 'Out on thee, seeming!', he proclaims piously (55), and laments that her outward beauty is in sharp contrast to her dissolute thoughts and feelings (101–2). Histrionically, he demands of Leonato, in a string of rhetorical questions, 'Leonato, stand I here? / Is this the prince? Is this the prince's brother? / Is this face Hero's? Are our eyes our own?' (69–71). In a catechism of Hero, he presses her to reveal the identity of the man she was talking to from her window the previous night. When Hero answers that no such conversation took place, Don Pedro triumphantly brandishes her response as a second piece of evidence for her sexual misconduct: 'Why, then are you no maiden' (87).

The line of reasoning of Claudio and Don Pedro is spurious, to say the least. On the one hand, they cite Hero's appearance of innocence as a lie, a sign of her play-acting. On the other hand, they insist on the evidence of their own eyes. These contradictory positions towards appearances and reality reverberate throughout the following speeches. Leonato echoes the words of Claudio almost verbatim. 'Why, doth not every earthly thing / Cry shame upon her? Could she deny / The story that is printed in her blood?' (120–2). Hero's blush marks her as guilty since, in a second layer of meaning, every woman carries the trace of woman's fallen state in her body. Eve, the first woman, was the first to sin, tempting Adam to join her in eating of the forbidden fruit in the Garden of Paradise. Like Don Pedro, Leonato immediately turns an unremarkable piece of information, namely the disclosure that Beatrice did not share Hero's bedchamber on the night in question, into a point scored for the prosecution: 'Confirmed, confirmed! O, that is stronger made / Which was before barred up with ribs of iron' (150–1). The irrefutable proof of Hero's guilt has only been further reinforced, he claims. When the Friar tries to defend Hero, Leonato asks, 'Why seek'st thou then to cover with excuse / That which appears in proper nakedness?' (174–5), stressing that the naked, unadorned truth is that Hero is guilty; every attempt to find other arguments is a false covering. But the Friar has an alternative theory to explain Hero's blushes. He has been watching her carefully.

> I have marked
> A thousand blushing apparitions
> To start into her face, a thousand innocent shames
> In angel whiteness beat away those blushes;
> And in her eye there hath appeared a fire
> To burn the errors that these princes hold
> Against her maiden truth.
>
> (158–64)

What the Friar has observed is the quick alternation of colour in Hero's face. Her blushes compete with paleness, an indisputable sign of innocence, white being associated with angels. This impression is reinforced by her flashing eyes, which, in a metaphor taken from religious persecution, contain a fire that would burn the heretical beliefs of Claudio and Don Pedro at the stake. The analogy is to false professions of faith that dare to impugn the verity of the true religion – her virginity. The Friar's syntax is complex, and he transposes nouns and adverbs, as early moderns frequently did – the truth he refers to is not 'maiden', but the truth of Hero's maidenhood. Still, the meaning of what he says is clear: Hero's changing colour is a symptom of her 'innocent shame', that is, shame linked to bashfulness, not to guilt. He supports his argument by drawing attention to his careful scrutiny of Hero, his long experience, his age and his vocation as a man of the cloth, all of which lend weight to his conclusion that Hero is innocent.

While the Friar's case is more congenial to us, since we are aware of the fact that Hero has been the victim of a conspiracy, it is nevertheless true that his reasoning is just as fallacious as is that of the two self-righteous noblemen. His conviction of her blamelessness is grounded on her appearance. Similarly, the Count draws his own conclusions from her aspect – albeit his verdict is the exact opposite of the Friar's. For Don Pedro and Count Claudio, the visual evidence of the window show remains incontrovertible. As the Prince asserts to Leonato when he next encounters the old man, 'she was charged with nothing / But what was true and very full of proof' (5.1.104–5). Neither the Friar nor Hero's accusers seem to entertain any doubt about the reliability of their perception, even though the play has already amply demonstrated the fallibility of trusting to visual impressions or hearsay. When Claudio hears the confession of Borachio and learns that Hero is guiltless, he announces, 'Sweet Hero! Now thy image doth appear / In the rare semblance that I loved it first' (5.1.241–2). Ironically, his words echo his categorical denunciation of Hero in the church scene as 'but the sign and semblance of her honour' (4.1.31). Now the vision that comes to his mind is that of her lovely ('rare') appearance, whose looks correspond to her essence; previously, he had labelled her outward aspect as a false front covering a polluted core. He has simply replaced one reading of Hero (as a whore) by another (as an angel). From the catastrophe he has unleashed he has learned nothing (Callaghan 2013: 141). Leonato, too, remains in the grip of the delusion that he can judge people on the grounds of what they look like. Confronted with one of the chief culprits who has caused such immeasurable pain to his daughter, Borachio, and his companion, Conrade, he demands, 'Which is the villain? Let me see his eyes, / That when I note another man like him / I may avoid him. Which of these is he?' (5.1.249–51). He still believes that by means of 'noting' he will be able to detect a villain. But he undermines his own allegation by being unable to deduce from their exterior which of two men is the delinquent.

Appearances and power

Much Ado About Nothing presents a superficial society that prizes stylish exteriors and surface impressions. Accordingly, its characters are easily swayed to misconstrue what they see or hear as corresponding to the truth. However, there are also a number of characters who relish manipulating appearances and engineering other people into behaving as they wish. Foremost amongst them are the princely brothers from Aragon, Don Pedro and Don John. Although the former is the legitimate ruler, the latter a bastard, and the former benign in his intentions, the latter malevolent, the play takes care to unsettle the apparent differences between them, both through the parallels in language (in the use of the term 'fashion') and in the juxtaposition of scenes. What the brothers share is a pleasure in deploying theatrical devices as a tool of power.

When Claudio first confesses to his superior, Don Pedro, that he is eager to win Hero as a bride, the Prince takes the words out of his mouth. He teases the young man that he is already turning into a loquacious lover, and apt to 'tire the hearer with a book of words' (1.1.288). He briskly proposes that he himself will arrange the marriage, and will speak to Hero and her father on the behalf of his companion. Claudio begins to tender his thanks, but once again, the Prince cuts him short. Then he makes a rather odd suggestion. Not content with merely engineering the alliance, he outlines a plan of action that will involve staging a little drama in which he will play the part of Claudio and court Hero in disguise. The text is silent about Claudio's reaction to Don Pedro's brainchild. In performances of the play, Claudio is sometimes presented as listening to the Prince with a furrowed brow, or gazing at him in surprise. But the text registers no protest on his part.

Once this piece of theatre has played itself out and the chain of misunderstandings has been cleared up, Don Pedro finds himself with time on his hands. He resolves to begin a larger project. With no false modesty, he compares himself to the ancient hero Hercules, and announces to his followers 'I will ... undertake one of Hercules' labours, which is to bring Signor Benedick and the Lady Beatrice into a mountain of affection th'one with th'other' (2.1.336–9). He proceeds to give directions for two playlets, one to gull Benedick and one to gull Beatrice. As he promises his assistants, 'If we can do this, Cupid is no longer an archer; his glory shall be ours, for we are the only love-gods' (355–7). 'Only' at the time could mean 'pre-eminent' as well as 'sole' (*OED* 2a and 3a). The analogy he draws to the mythological god of love is telling – he regards it as his god-like prerogative to orchestrate the affairs of his subjects. In point of fact, he is vying with the gods in exerting control over the lives of others, and is determined to outdo them. Like a stage director, he gives his co-conspirators detailed instructions about their roles, and uses explicitly theatrical imagery to describe the stupefied response of the victims: 'That's the scene that I would see, which will be merely a dumb show' (2.3.210–11). A dumb show was a pantomime that often preceded a play; the word 'merely' meant 'completely'. Don Pedro's master plan for a drama is one in which the decisive words spoken will be his.

Skill at deceiving others does not mean that the characters are themselves immune to duplicity. Ironically, the Prince is fooled by another dramatic performance, the window show in which Borachio and Margaret mime Hero and a fictive lover. The performance is so convincing that Don John achieves his goal – to bring about a disastrous outcome of the wedding plans and a loss of face for his brother and his bosom companion, Claudio. In a brilliant analysis, Jean Howard has scrutinized the power relations in the play and has detected a rivalry between both brothers that is carried out with the instruments of theatricality. Both brothers attempt to manipulate the world through fictions, but Don John's show involves an assault on aristocratic status. He orchestrates a scenario in which Borachio and Margaret usurp the clothes, names and environment of their betters. The outrage of Don Pedro and Claudio is partly a reaction to the subversive implications of the substitution scene. Fittingly, the social upstarts are punished, along with the illegitimate brother. What the play reveals is that the connection between appearances and reality is also inflected by relations of power. Don Pedro's mastery of Messina is partly based on his control of theatrical devices; conversely, his playlets succeed partly because they are buttressed by his authority.

Don John flees Messina, but his brother, too, fades into the background at the end of the play. What the two Spanish noblemen also share is their outsider status. Don John is the generic scapegoat of comedy who needs to be expelled for the comic reconciliation to commence. After successfully engineering the marriage between Claudio and Hero and Beatrice and Benedick, Don Pedro lingers on the fringes of the festive society. 'Prince, thou art sad – get thee a wife, get thee a wife!' Benedick advises him (5.4.120). Don Pedro seems to have joined his brother in turning melancholy. Shakespeare's comedies often end with certain characters excluded from the charmed circle of the final festivity – Shylock in *The Merchant of Venice*, Jaques in *As You Like It*, Antonio, Malvolio and Feste in *Twelfth Night*. Having managed the lives of a handful of the leading citizens of Messina with energy and zest, at the end of the play Don Pedro falls silent.

The brothers from Aragon are not the only characters to manipulate appearances for their own ends. Claudio, Leonato and the Friar all attempt to wrest the meaning of Hero's blushes into evidence to support their belief in her guilt or innocence. The Friar's plan to salvage the reputation of Hero involves an elaborate fraud, a 'mourning ostentation' (4.1.205) or a show of mourning, which includes a false funeral. Leonato demands that the Prince and Claudio attend mourning rites to take place at the empty tomb of Hero, and arranges for a wedding ostensibly to a niece of his, in reality to his daughter, who appears masked until the ceremony has taken place. Even Leonato's display of grief is not quite what it seems. In Act 5 Scene 1, Leonato and Antonio challenge the two noblemen to a duel on the grounds of their having killed his daughter. In reality, as they know, she is sequestered somewhere, waiting for Claudio's change of heart, as the Friar proposed.

Delusion and self-delusion

Much Ado About Nothing does not explicitly endorse any of the philosophical views about being and seeming that we have discussed – the notion that there is no correlation between attractive exteriors and the truth, as posited by Plato in *Gorgias*, or the Ciceronian belief that outward appearances correspond with inner values, or the attitude of Machiavelli and Castiglione that inward truths are largely irrelevant. Nor does it refute them. Instead, the play seems to suggest that the truth is more complex. The play is riddled with examples of inaccurate judgement and misconstruction of the truth. But at a closer look, it emerges that very often the delusion the protagonists are subject to is inextricably bound up with their self-delusion. People see what they want to see and believe what they want to believe. Without collusion on the part of the duped, fraudulence would not be effective. Characters are deceived by chicanery because they are only too willing to entertain the ideas planted in their heads by the dissemblers – most blatantly, in the case of Hero's infidelity. Claudio is quick to believe that Hero has seduced the Prince to abandon loyalty to his friend, inspired by the belief that women are notorious temptresses. Claudio, Don Pedro and Leonato are more than receptive to the notion that Hero is unchaste, embedded as it is in a long tradition of suspicion of women. Benedick and Beatrice are happy to believe that the other is in love with them, driven perhaps by a mixture of loneliness, yearning for affection

and a generous portion of self-love. Dogberry and his
fellows are too obtuse to understand anything that is going
on. Nevertheless, they may well be influenced by suspicion
of those they deem social upstarts, such as 'Deformed', and
by uneasiness about any seemingly disrespectful comments
about those in the higher echelons of society. As for Hero's
blushing aspect, it seems to mean whatever the perceiver
wishes to read into it.

The Friar hopes that once Claudio hears Hero is dead,
his image of her will change, and he will begin to mourn her
departure and regret his cruelty. He explains,

> For so it falls out
> That what we have we prize not to the worth
> Whiles we enjoy it, but being lacked and lost,
> Why, then we rack the value, then we find
> The virtue that possession would not show us
> Whiles it was ours.
>
> (4.1.217–22)

The value of a possession, he suggests, is not intrinsic. It is
determined by the attitude of the human beings who own
the object, and who rate it higher if it is no longer in their
possession. Thus Claudio will begin to hold Hero dear after
her supposed death. As it happens, the play does not bear out
this optimistic opinion of Claudio. But what it does suggest is
that it is we who influence the meaning of appearances. It is
true that sometimes façades are radically incompatible with
the truth, as in the fraudulent window show, which dupes
Claudio and the Prince. Sometimes appearances correspond
to reality – for the members of the watch, Borachio looks
and sounds like a villain, and they are right, but for the
wrong reasons. They arrest Borachio and Conrade because
they mistakenly believe they are in cahoots with a thief called
'Deformed', who is a social imposter. In the cross-examination
of the prisoners, Dogberry accuses them of perjury (he
probably means slander) for denigrating Don John, and of

burglary for receiving money for participating in the window show. In effect, the lies Dogberry charges them with are the plain truth. In Dogberry's eyes, their greatest crime is to call him an ass – another truth the audience has no difficulty in accepting.

Sometimes, the play proposes, appearances actually create the reality they apparently depict – the gulling of Beatrice and Benedick results in their succumbing to the illusion of their being in love. In the play, love is not a matter of inner feeling, but above all a performance. It apparently consists in being preoccupied with one's appearance – fashionable attire, going to the barber, wearing perfume – or, with regard to Beatrice, allegedly staying up at night and writing letters to her love, sobbing and being distraught, and writing sonnets. It is these external signs that incriminate Beatrice and Benedick and prove even to themselves that they are in love. Whether or not the two protagonists are secretly in love all along, as some critics maintain, by the end of the play they have incorporated the lies put into circulation by their friends and have fallen in love with each other. Or so they believe.

Sometimes, however, things don't seem as clear cut. Does the shaming ritual Claudio is forced to undergo have any effect on him? He goes through the motions of mourning, but has he actually repented his harsh treatment of the woman he claims to love? The play provides no answer, although in some performances actors are at pains to display anguish in their facial expressions. The text suggests that in this case, Machiavelli's solution might be apposite. We have no insight into the inward self of others, and the play offers us no purchase on Claudio's real feelings. But perhaps it is irrelevant how he feels. What matters is that he is forced to demonstrate remorse. For our social life, performance might have a value that has little to do with inner truth.

Metatheatricality

Lastly, the play puts forward the proposition that sometimes surfaces might simply create pleasure, quite irrespective of the truth they may or may not reflect. In this way, *Much Ado About Nothing* might be as much about aesthetic illusions as about the events in Messina. The play explores the power of appearances by means of the trope of theatricality, and includes the theatre itself in its reflections. Aspects of a play that draw attention to its very nature as drama are known as *metadrama* or *metatheatricality*. *Much Ado About Nothing* is brimming with playlets and stage manager figures manipulating appearances, with people wearing masks and playacting to each other, and other characters watching them. Some of these moments are, for instance, the masque, the ritual mourning of Hero and the final marriage with the masked Hero. The play abounds in metatheatrical in-jokes and comments, which foreground the fact that we are in the theatre watching a play. We have already mentioned the remark Antonio makes during the masque about his counterfeiting himself – which is a clever metatheatrical joke, since everyone on stage is counterfeiting their characters. This quip is repeated in the gulling of Benedick in a hilarious little exchange between the conspirators. Talking about Beatrice, they pretend to wonder whether she is really in love with Benedick, or only shamming.

DON PEDRO
   Maybe she doth but counterfeit.
CLAUDIO
   Faith, like enough.
LEONATO
   O God! Counterfeit? There was never counterfeit
   of passion came so near the life of passion as she
   discovers it.

                                                    (2.3.104–8)

Leonato denies that Beatrice is only playacting – and at the same time offers a handsome compliment to the boy actor playing the role, declaring that never had the pretence of love been depicted in so life-like a manner. Another metatheatrical remark in the same scene is made by Benedick to the audience, in an aside, which in itself is a metadramatic device and breaks the illusion that the events presented on stage are a slice of real life. Benedick wonders whether or not to believe the three schemers. He decides that although the dialogue is dubious he cannot believe that a man of such venerable aspect as Leonato could be involved in a deception: 'I should think this is a gull, but that the white-bearded fellow speaks it. Knavery cannot, sure, hide himself in such reverence' (119–21). What makes the remark so funny is the fact that 'the white-bearded fellow' is, of course, an actor, someone in the business of deception. Other examples of metatheatrical jokes are, for instance, Beatrice's nudge to Claudio when he is dumbstruck at hearing that the Prince has wooed and won Hero for him: 'Speak, Count, 'tis your cue' (2.1.280). Benedick makes a similar wisecrack when fooling around with Claudio and Don Pedro in the first scene of the play. He gleefully spills the beans about Claudio's newly confessed infatuation with Hero to the Prince: 'he is in love. With who? Now, that is your grace's part' (1.1.198–9). These words, like the previous words of Beatrice, are in fact the cues that the actors playing the parts would have learnt. One last example of metatheatricality in action must suffice. Before Hero and Ursula begin to gull Beatrice in earnest, Ursula tells us, 'So angle we for Beatrice, who even now / Is couched in the woodbine coverture' (3.1.29–30). The play self-consciously highlights the action that is about to commence by characters who briefly slip out of their roles to talk to us as actors to audience members.

To sum up: the play explores the vexed issue of how appearances and surface impressions relate to the truth from a variety of perspectives. Sometimes façades are fraudulent, sometimes they correlate with reality, whether inadvertently or not. Manipulating appearances is also a matter of who controls illusions in a given society. Nevertheless, delusion is closely intertwined with self-delusion – people perceive what they are willing to see. Sometimes, the play suggests, appearances actually create the reality they supposedly depict, as in the case of Beatrice and Benedick – falling in love might well be a matter of wanting to fall in love. Some surfaces, however, such as the wit with which the play is spangled, simply create aesthetic pleasure.

In a play thronged with references to staged performances and playacting, all these aspects might reflect on the theatre as well. Watching the power of illusions on others might make us muse about our own relation to appearances, and our own susceptibility to images. And it might make us wonder whether we too are social performers, created through our performances.

Writing matters

1　Discuss the relation between the pairs of lovers, Claudio and Hero and Benedick and Beatrice. One significant factor, for instance, is that Claudio and Hero are never alone on stage. Are there other interesting elements that are worth taking a closer look at?

2　In connection with the theme of appearances, perhaps you might like to ponder why Shakespeare does not stage the window show, a topic that we have only very briefly touched upon. If you were producing the play, would you stage it or not?

3　Compare Beatrice and Benedick to other famous Shakespearean lovers, not only in the comedies, but in the tragedies, too. Othello and Desdemona spring to mind, or the Macbeths, or Antony and Cleopatra. Discuss two sets of couples in terms of their dialogues with each other. Do the relationships undergo a change in the course of each play?

4 In which other plays does honour or dishonour play a role? There are surprising affinities between *Much Ado About Nothing* and a play like *Julius Caesar*, where family honour and reputation play a role in persuading Brutus to join the conspiracy. Similarly, Portia is swayed by considerations of honour. Perhaps you can think of other plays where honour and glory, and the shame of dishonour, are decisive.

5 Seeming and being are of course themes with which Shakespeare was concerned throughout his career. Can you think of other plays that might fruitfully be juxtaposed with *Much Ado About Nothing* in relation to how each play tackles the theme? Manipulation of appearances is Iago's forte, too. It might be interesting to compare Iago and the interior dramatists of *Much Ado About Nothing* in terms of their dramaturgical strategies.

6 Look for further examples of metatheatricality in the play. Alternatively, take a look at the use of metatheatricality in other plays, for instance, plays-within-plays in *A Midsummer Night's Dream* or *Hamlet*. How does each play explore the question of theatrical illusion?

CHAPTER FOUR

Language, performance and writing

Performance criticism

Throughout this book we have focused on the written text of the play and on the way it has been shaped by historical and cultural conditions and the theatrical conventions of its time. Many of us, however, will first have access to a Shakespearean play through a performance, either on stage or on film. Indeed, some critics argue that a play is like a musical script – it only really exists when it is performed. This argument corresponds to a radical shift away from earlier generations of critics, especially a school of literary criticism that held sway roughly from the 1920s to the 1970s known as the New Criticism or Formalism. New Critics were solely concerned with the words of a text. They ignored all extraneous elements, including performance, as irrelevant. They especially rejected those even earlier critics who often approached a play from a biographical viewpoint, attempting to ferret out information about the playwright from the text, or, conversely, reading details of Shakespeare's life into the play. Some critics were entirely concerned with characters, whom they discussed as if they were real people, not fictive artefacts. Alternatively, histori-cally minded critics read plays as straightforward reflections of historical events. As might have become clear in the course of reading this book, we have tried to adopt what might be seen as a New Historicist angle, regarding texts as inevitably influenced by historical and cultural developments (such as the Renaissance cult of honour), yet attempting to do justice to the often contradictory cross-currents that existed at every historical period. Furthermore, we have tried to show that *Much Ado About Nothing* does not simply mirror prevailing ways of thought in early modern England – ways of thinking about dishonour, the role of women and ideal relationships between lovers, for example – but in many ways offers a different take on dominant cultural codes.

New Critics have taught us many valuable lessons and in this book we have tried to incorporate their rigorous attention to the words of a text in the way we have looked at the language of the play. However, in the past few decades the idea that early modern stage conditions had a decisive influence on the meaning of Shakespeare's plays has increasingly gained momentum. But does this signify that we can slip into the minds of Elizabethan spectators and see the play with their eyes? And what does it imply for film or stage versions produced in the twenty-first century? Are they only legitimate if they faithfully reproduce the conventions of the Renaissance theatre? For a start, this would mean no roles for actresses. And if we only respond to the play in performance, what value does a close study of the words of the text have?

These are questions for each of us to grapple with, but it might be helpful to look at what a leading performance critic, W. B. Worthen, has to say. In a seminal essay entitled 'Deeper Meanings and Theatrical Technique: The Rhetoric of Perfomance Criticism' (1989), he warns us against falling into the trap of entirely dismissing the value of a close reading of the text and celebrating performance as the only way of gaining a purchase on a play. For one thing, as he reminds us, performance changes over time. Performances too are shaped by the conventions of acting in a given culture, by the gender norms and the conceptions of human identity that are current at a particular time. Even if we try to reproduce the exact conditions of Shakespeare's theatre, this doesn't imply we can retrieve the inherent meaning of the text. Performances don't simply translate the words on the page on to the stage – they *produce* a specific version of the text. All performances are interpretations, just as all articles or books written by literary critics are interpretations. They just use divergent tools to convey their reading of the play. In fact, Worthen claims that we ought to regard all methods of engaging with a text as a performance. Reading, literary criticism and staging a play are all different ways of performing a text, or producing a certain version of a text.

We have already made a few suggestions about issues worth taking a close look at in connection with the written language of *Much Ado About Nothing*. Let us turn to a couple of performances and see what questions might be interesting to pursue. There have been two popular film versions of the play: one directed by Kenneth Branagh, which was first screened in 1993, and a film set in contemporary California produced by Joss Whedon in 2012. In addition, there are film versions of a theatre production by Shakespeare's Globe in 2012, directed by Jeremy Herrin, and a production by the Royal Shakespeare Company in 2015, directed by Christopher Luscombe. The latter production was whimsically called *Love's Labour's Won*, after the lost play by Shakespeare, and was staged in tandem with a production of *Love's Labour's Lost*.

Film and stage performances

The question at the heart of the relationship between a Shakespearean play and film is how the elaborate language of the play might be translated into the realist medium of film. Critics have traditionally distinguished between the **theatrical** mode, the **realist** mode and the **filmic** mode of Shakespearean films (Shaughnessy 1998). The first would include film versions of stage productions, the second realistic portrayals of the narrative of the play, and the third would exploit the potential of film to create visual poetry. It might be useful to reflect whether in the case of the films of *Much Ado About Nothing* these distinctions really hold.

1   Branagh's film, studded with famous theatre actors and film stars, was financially one of the most successful Shakespeare films ever produced. No doubt the spectacular setting in a Tuscan villa and the superb performances by an array of attractive actors contributed to its success. Branagh faithfully adheres to the words of the text. However, like every director, he cuts many of the lines. It might be interesting to closely monitor the scenes of the film and compare them with the play. Is there a pattern in the **editing**? Does it change anything about the way the story comes across? Look, for instance, at the theme of misunderstanding. What happens to the snarl of misapprehension in the plot? What does Branagh do with the most unpleasant lines of the characters? The film evokes the sense of an alluring, sun-drenched world. What happens to the darker sides of the play?

2   One of the strengths of film is its ability to produce a realist representation of the setting. How do the directors use filmic means to visualize **space**? Are the Tuscan villa and the luxurious Californian estate clever ways of transporting Messina into the world of film? How do the films, particularly Whedon's, create the impression of a society that sets a premium on style and fashion?

3   Whedon uses the device of flashback to create a backstory for Benedick and Beatrice. Is this an ingenious way of introducing **time** into the narrative, or is it unnecessary? Is something gained, and something lost? If so, what?

4 We mentioned the notion that early modern audiences were keenly attuned to detecting aural signals such as the change from prose to verse and vice versa. One technique that film has at its disposal that Shakespeare's theatre did not is background music and **sound effects**. How are they deployed in either film?

5 A central instrument in film is **montage**. Look carefully at the juxtaposition of images in either film. Do they correlate with the structural symmetries we have observed in the play? Do the films succeed in adding further layers of meaning to the play?

6 In all four performances, look at the choices of the productions in terms of **setting, props, costume** and **spatial arrangements**. Luscombe, for instance, sets the two plays, *Love's Labour's Lost* and *Much Ado About Nothing*, in the period immediately before and after the First World War. Does this setting enrich a reading of the play, or does it seem misguided?

7 How do the film and stage productions present the main protagonists? How do they deal with the disagreeable aspects of Claudio's **character**?

8 How do they convey the **themes** of the play to modern audiences? Look, for instance, at Whedon's use of surveillance cameras and mirrors to create a visual correlative for the issue of 'noting'. How do the productions deal with the background of an honour culture?

9 What strategies do the productions, both film and stage, employ to convey the **humour** of the play to modern audiences? As we have seen, many of the jokes (cuckoldry jests, malapropism with words with which we are unfamiliar) need to be explained to a contemporary reader. One strategy performances use is to find alternative sources of comedy, for example by adding comic business or horseplay to compensate for jokes that fall flat. What choices do these productions make?

10   Finally, it might be fruitful to delve into the performance history of the play. Critics such as Penny Gay have done extensive research on the various stage productions of the play and traced the changing representation in particular of the relationship between Beatrice and Benedick. You might like to think about how recent productions relate to the staging history of *Much Ado About Nothing*.

These are just a few suggestions about avenues to explore. Lastly, here are a couple of additional tips for writing an essay. Other volumes in this series have dealt with this topic extensively, so allow me simply to add a few points that might be worth repeating.

Writing a research paper

- Organize your ideas in logical steps. Your paper should have an introduction and a conclusion flanking the main body of your text.

- Do not give an impressionistic presentation of your thoughts. Instead, remember you are arguing a case and attempting to persuade the reader. This means you need to support all your statements with evidence from the text.

- Select a few key passages and/or quotations around which you can build your argument.

- Always comment on the quotations. Do not make the mistake of thinking the quotation speaks for itself.

- Do not paraphrase the text.

- Use secondary material only in support of your arguments – don't allow it to overshadow your own ideas. However, you should be aware of the current state of discussion in the field of scholarship.

- As regards style, try to be concise, precise, clear and objective.

- Most importantly, be open to contradictions in a text, or jarring notes. If something seems to strike a wrong note to you, it might well be rewarding to pursue your hunch. Texts often contain contradictory strands of meaning, like the title of the play. It is exploring this diversity of nuances that makes the work of literary criticism so enriching.

BIBLIOGRAPHY

Selected criticism of *Much Ado About Nothing*

Berger, Harry Jr. 'Against the Sink-a-Pace: Sexual and Family Politics in *Much Ado About Nothing*'. *Much Ado About Nothing and The Taming of the Shrew: Contemporary Critical Essays*, ed. Marion Wynne-Davis. New Casebooks. Basingstoke: Palgrave Macmillan, 2001, 13–30.

Berry, Ralph. *Shakespeare's Comedies: Explorations in Form*. Princeton: Princeton University Press, 1972, 154–74.

Berry, Ralph. *Shakespeare and Social Class*. Atlantic Highlands, NJ: Humanities Press International, 1989, 56–61.

Cerasano, S. R. 'Half a Dozen Dangerous Words'. *Much Ado About Nothing and The Taming of the Shrew: Contemporary Critical Essays*, ed. Marion Wynne-Davis. New Casebooks. Basingstoke: Palgrave Macmillan, 2001, 31–50.

Collington, Philip D. '"Stuffed with all Honourable Virtues": *Much Ado About Nothing* and *The Book of the Courtier*'. *Studies in Philology* 103 (3) (2006): 281–321.

Cook, Carol. '"The Sign and Semblance of Her Honor": Reading Gender Difference in *Much Ado About Nothing*'. *Shakespeare and Gender: A History*, ed. Deborah Barker and Ivo Kamps. New York: Verso, 1995, 75–103.

Dawson, Anthony. 'Much Ado About Signifying'. *Studies in English Literature, 1500–1900* 2 (2) (1982): 211–21.

Dillon, Janette. Introduction. *Much Ado About Nothing*, ed. R. A. Foakes. The Penguin Shakespeare. London: Penguin, 2005, xxi–lvii.

Evans, Bertrand. 'Awareness and Unawareness in *Much Ado About Nothing*'. *Shakespeare's Comedies: An Anthology of Modern Criticism*, ed. Laurence Lerner. Harmondsworth: Penguin, 1967, 197–218.

Everett, Barbara. 'Something of Great Constancy'. *Shakespeare: Much Ado About Nothing and As You Like It*, ed. John Russell Brown. A Casebook. Basingstoke: Macmillan, 1979, 94–116.

Everett, Barbara. '*Much Ado About Nothing*: The Unsociable Comedy'. *Much Ado About Nothing and The Taming of the Shrew: Contemporary Critical Essays*, ed. Marion Wynne-Davis. New Casebooks. Basingstoke: Palgrave Macmillan, 2001, 51–68.

Foakes, R. A. 'The Owl and the Cuckoo: Voices of Maturity in Shakespeare's Comedies'. *Shakespearian Comedy*, ed. J. R. Brown and B. Harris. Stratford-upon-Avon Studies 14. London: Edward Arnold, 1972, 121–41.

Gay, Penny. '*Much Ado About Nothing*: A Kind of Merry War'. *Much Ado About Nothing and The Taming of the Shrew: Contemporary Critical Essays*, ed. Marion Wynne-Davis. New Casebooks. Basingstoke: Palgrave Macmillan, 2001, 69–102.

Greenblatt, Stephen. '*Much Ado About Nothing*'. *The Norton Shakespeare: Comedies*, ed. Stephen Greenblatt, Walter Cohen, Jean E. Howard and Katharine Eisaman Maus, 2nd edn. New York: W. W. Norton, 2008, 557–65.

Howard, Jean. E. 'Antitheatricality Staged: The Workings of Ideology in Shakespeare's *Much Ado About Nothing*'. *Much Ado About Nothing and The Taming of the Shrew: Contemporary Critical Essays*, ed. Marion Wynne-Davis. New Casebooks. Basingstoke: Palgrave Macmillan, 2001, 103–22.

Huston, J. Dennis. *Shakespeare's Comedies of Play*. Basingstoke: Palgrave Macmillan, 1981.

Legatt, Alexander. *Shakespeare's Comedy of Love*. London: Methuen, 1974, 151–83.

Mangan, Michael. *A Preface to Shakespeare's Comedies: 1594–1603*. London: Routledge, 1996, 179–201.

Mares, F. H. 'Introduction'. *Much Ado About Nothing*, ed. F. H. Mares. The New Cambridge Shakespeare. Cambridge: Cambridge University Press, 2003, 1–59.

Mason, Pamela. *Much Ado About Nothing*. Text and Performance. Basingstoke: Macmillan, 1992.

McEachern, Claire. 'Introduction'. *Much Ado about Nothing*, ed. Claire McEachern. The Arden Shakespeare, 3rd series, rev. edn. London: Bloomsbury Arden Shakespeare, 2016, 1–151.

Mulryne, J. R. 'The Large Design'. *Shakespeare: Much Ado*

About Nothing and As You Like It, ed. John Russell Brown. A
   Casebook. Basingstoke: Macmillan, 1979, 117–29.
Mueschke, Paul and Miriam Mueschke. 'Illusion and
   Metamorphosis'. *Shakespeare: Much Ado About Nothing
   and As You Like It*, ed. John Russell Brown. A Casebook.
   Basingstoke: Macmillan, 1979, 130–48.
Neely, Carol Thomas. 'Broken Nuptials: *Much Ado about
   Nothing*'. *Shakespeare's Comedies*, ed. Gary Waller. Longman
   Critical Readers. London: Longman, 1991, 139–54.
Rossiter, A. P. '*Much Ado About Nothing*'. *Shakespeare's Comedies:
   An Anthology of Modern Criticism*, ed. Laurence Lerner.
   Harmondsworth: Penguin, 1967, 181–96.
Ryan, Kiernan. '"Strange Misprision": *Much Ado About Nothing*'.
   Shakespeare's Comedies. Basingstoke: Palgrave Macmillan,
   2009, 164–97.
Scott, Mary Augusta. '*The Book of the Courtyer*: A Possible Source
   of Benedick and Beatrice'. *PMLA* 16 (4) (1901): 475–502.
Slights, Camille Wells. 'The Unauthorized Language of *Much
   Ado About Nothing*'. *Shakespeare's Comic Commonwealths*.
   Toronto: University of Toronto Press, 1993, 171–89.
Stauffer, Donald A. 'Words and Actions'. *Shakespeare: Much Ado
   About Nothing and As You Like It*, ed. John Russell Brown.
   A Casebook. Basingstoke: Macmillan, 1979, 87–93.
Trewin, J. C. '*Much Ado About Nothing* in the Theatre'.
   Shakespeare's Comedies: An Anthology of Modern Criticism, ed.
   Laurence Lerner. Harmondsworth: Penguin, 1967, 219–23.
Zitner, Sheldon P. 'General Introduction'. *Much Ado About
   Nothing*, ed. Sheldon P. Zitner. The Oxford Shakespeare.
   Oxford: Oxford University Press, 1993, 1–78.

FURTHER READING

Primary sources

Aristotle. *Politics*, trans. H. Rackam. Loeb Classical Library. Cambridge, MA: Harvard University Press, 1932.

Aristotle. *Art of Rhetoric*, trans. John Henry Freese. Loeb Classical Library. Cambridge, MA: Harvard University Press, 2008.

Aristotle. *The Nicomachean Ethics*, trans. David Ross. Oxford World's Classics. Oxford: Oxford University Press, 2009.

Ascham, Roger. *The Schoolmaster* (1570), ed. Lawrence V. Ryan. Folger Documents of Tudor and Stuart Civilization. Ithaca, NY: Cornell University Press, 1967.

Castiglione, Baldesar. *The Book of the Courtier*, trans. Charles S. Singleton, ed. Daniel Javitch. A Norton Critical Edition. New York: W. W. Norton, 2002.

Cicero. *On Obligations*, trans. P. G. Walsh. Oxford World's Classics. Oxford: Oxford University Press, 2000.

Cicero. *On the Ideal Orator*, trans. James M. May and Jakob Wisse. Oxford: Oxford University Press, 2001.

Florio, John. *Florio's Second Frutes*, 1591.

Guazzo, Stefano. *The Civile Conversation of M. Steeven Guazzo*, trans. George Pettie and Bartholomew Young, 1586 [1581].

Lyly, John. *Euphues: The Anatomy of Wit* and *Euphues and His England*, ed. Leah Scragg. The Revel Plays. Manchester: Manchester University Press, 2009.

Machiavelli. *The Prince*, trans. Russell Price, ed. Quentin Skinner and Russell Price. Cambridge Texts in the History of Political Thought. Cambridge: Cambridge University Press, 1988.

Plato. *Symposium*, trans. W. R. M. Lamb. Loeb Classical Library. Cambridge, MA: Harvard University Press, 1925.

Plato. *Gorgias*, trans. W. R. M. Lamb. Loeb Classical Library. Cambridge, MA: Harvard University Press, 1983.

Quintilian. *The Orator's Education*, trans. Donald A. Russell,

5 vols. Loeb Classical Library. Cambridge, MA: Harvard University Press, 2001.

Stubbes, Philip. *The Anatomie of Abuses*. Reprinted from the 3rd edn of 1585 under the superintendence of William B. D. D. Turnbull. London: Pickering, 1836.

Secondary sources

Adelman, Janet. *Suffocating Mothers: Fantasies of Maternal Origin in Shakespeare's Plays, 'Hamlet' to 'The Tempest'*. London: Routledge, 1992.

Altman, Joel B. *The Tudor Play of Mind: Rhetorical Inquiry and the Development of Elizabethan Drama*. Berkeley: University of California Press, 1978.

Amussen, Susan Dwyer. *An Ordered Society: Gender and Class in Early Modern England*. New York: Columbia University Press, 1988.

Anglo, Sydney. *Machiavelli – the First Century: Studies in Enthusiasm, Hostility, and Irrelevance*. Oxford: Oxford University Press, 2005.

Appiah, Kwame Anthony. *The Honor Code: How Moral Revolutions Happen*. New York: W. W. Norton, 2010.

Ascoli, Albert Russell and Victoria Kahn, eds. *Machiavelli and the Discourse of Literature*. Ithaca, NY: Cornell University Press, 1993.

Barber, C. L. *Shakespeare's Festive Comedy: A Study of Dramatic Form and its Relations to Social Custom*. Princeton, NJ: Princeton University Press, 1972.

Bate, Jonathan. *The Genius of Shakespeare*. London: Picador, 1997.

Berger, Harry, Jr. *The Absence of Grace: Sprezzatura and Suspicion in Two Renaissance Courtesy Books*. Stanford: Stanford University Press, 2000.

Bergson, Henri. 'Laughter'. *Comedy*, ed. Wylie Sypher. Baltimore: The Johns Hopkins University Press, 1956, 61–190.

Bryson, Anne. *From Courtesy to Civility: Changing Codes of Conduct in Early Modern England*. Oxford: Clarendon, 1998.

Bullough, Geoffrey. *Narrative and Dramatic Sources of*

Shakespeare. Volume 2: The Comedies. Edinburgh: Edinburgh University Press, 1958.

Burckhardt, Jacob. *The Civilization of the Renaissance in Italy*, trans. S. G. C. Middlemore. 1860. London: Penguin, 1990.

Burke, Peter. *Popular Culture in Early Modern Europe*. London: Temple Smith, 1978.

Burke, Peter. *The Renaissance*. Studies in European History. Atlantic Highlands, NJ: Humanities Press International, 1987.

Burke, Peter. *The Fortunes of the Courtier: The European Reception of Castiglione's* Courtegiano. University Park, PA: Pennsylvania State University, Press, 1995.

Callaghan, Dympna. *Who Was William Shakespeare? An Introduction to the Life and Works*. Oxford: Wiley-Blackwell, 2013.

Chambers, E. K. *The Elizabethan Stage*, 4 vols. Oxford: Clarendon Press, 1923.

Danson, Lawrence. *Shakespeare's Dramatic Genres*. Oxford Shakespeare Topics. Oxford: Oxford University Press, 2000.

Dawson, Anthony B. and Paul Yachnin. *The Culture of Playgoing in Shakespeare's England: A Collaborative Debate*. Cambridge: Cambridge University Press, 2001.

Elias, Norbert. *The Civilising Process: The History of Manners and State Formation and Civilization*, trans. Edmund Jephcott. 1939. Oxford: Blackwell, 1994.

Enterline, Lynn. *Shakespeare's Schoolroom: Rhetoric, Discipline, Emotion*. Philadelphia, PA: Pennsylvania University Press, 2012.

Es, Bart Van. *Shakespeare in Company*. Oxford: Oxford University Press, 2013.

Fletcher, Anthony. *Gender, Sex and Subordination in England 1500–1800*. New Haven: Yale University Press, 1995.

Fox, Alistair. *The English Renaissance: Identity and Representation in Elizabethan England*. Oxford: Blackwell, 1997.

Frye, Herman Northrop. *Anatomy of Criticism: Four Essays*. Princeton: Princeton University Press, 1957.

Ghose, Indira. *Shakespeare and Laughter*. Manchester: Manchester University Press, 2008.

Grazia, Margreta de and Stanley Wells, eds. *The New Cambridge Companion to Shakespeare*. Cambridge: Cambridge University Press, 2010.

Gurr, Andrew. *The Shakespearean Stage, 1574–1642*. Cambridge: Cambridge University Press, 1992.

Hanning, Robert W. and David Rosand, eds. *Castiglione: The Ideal and the Real in Renaissance Culture*. New Haven: Yale University Press, 1983.

Hawkes, David. *Idols of the Marketplace: Idolatry and Commodity Fetishism in English Literature, 1580–1680*. New York: Palgrave, 2001.

Hoeniger, David F. *Medicine and Shakespeare in the English Renaissance*. Newark: University of Delaware Press, 1992.

Hull, Suzanne E. *Chaste, Silent and Obedient: English Books for Women, 1475–1640*. San Marino: Huntington Library, 1982.

Hutton, Ronald. *The Rise and Fall of Merry England: The Ritual Year 1400–1700*. Oxford: Oxford University Press, 1994.

James, Mervyn. 'English Politics and the Concept of Honour, 1485–1642'. *Society, Politics and Culture: Studies in Early Modern England*. Cambridge: Cambridge University Press, 1986, 308–415.

Johnson, Samuel. 'Preface'. *The Plays of William Shakespeare: Selected Poetry and Prose*, ed. Frank Brody and W. K. Wimsatt. Berkeley: University of California Press, 1977, 299–336.

Jones, Ann Rosalind and Peter Stallybrass. *Renaissance Clothing and the Materials of Memory*. Cambridge: Cambridge University Press, 2000.

Kahn, Victoria. *Machiavellian Rhetoric: From the Counter-Reformation to Milton*. Princeton, NJ: Princeton University Press, 1994.

Kelso, Ruth. *Doctrine for the Lady of the Renaissance*. Urbana: University of Illinois Press, 1956.

Kelso, Ruth. *The Doctrine of the English Gentleman in the Sixteenth Century*. Gloucester, MA: Peter Smith, 1964.

Kennedy, George. *The Art of Rhetoric in the Roman World, 300 B.C.–A.D. 300*. Princeton, NJ: Princeton University Press, 1972.

Kermode, Frank. *Shakespeare's Language*. London: Penguin, 2001.

Kinney, Arthur F. 'Rhetoric and Fiction in Elizabethan England'. *Renaissance Eloquence: Studies in the Theory and Practice of Renaissance Rhetoric*, ed. James J. Murphy. Berkeley: University of California Press, 1983, 385–93.

Kinney, Arthur F. *Continental Humanist Poetics: Studies in Erasmus, Castiglione, Marguerite de Navarre, Rabelais, and Cervantes*. Amherst: University of Massachusetts, 1989, 87–134.

Lanham, Richard A. *The Motives of Eloquence: Literary Rhetoric in the Renaissance*. New Haven: Yale University Press, 1976.

Lanham, Richard A. *A Handlist of Rhetorical Terms*. Berkeley: University of California Press, 1991.

Leggatt, Alexander, ed. *The Cambridge Companion to Shakespearean Comedy*. Cambridge: Cambridge University Press, 2002.

Mack, Peter. *Elizabethan Rhetoric: Theory and Practice*. Cambridge: Cambridge University Press, 2002.

Maguire, Laurie and Emma Smith. *Thirty Great Myths About Shakespeare*. Oxford: Wiley-Blackwell, 2013.

McAlindon, Thomas. *Shakespeare and Decorum*. London: Macmillan, 1973.

McDonald, Russ. *Shakespeare and the Arts of Language*. Oxford Shakespeare Topics. Oxford: Oxford University Press, 2001.

Miola, Robert S. *Shakespeare's Reading*. Oxford Shakespeare Topics. Oxford: Oxford University Press, 2000.

Muir, Kenneth. *The Sources of Shakespeare's Plays*. London: Methuen, 1977.

Najemy, John M., ed. *The Cambridge Companion to Machiavelli*. Cambridge: Cambridge University Press, 2010.

Nelson, T. G. A. *Comedy: The Theory of Comedy in Literature, Drama, and Cinema*. Oxford: Oxford University Press, 1990.

Newman, Karen. *Fashioning Femininity and English Renaissance Drama*. Chicago: University of Chicago Press, 1991.

Palfrey, Simon. *Doing Shakespeare*. London: Arden Shakespeare, 2005.

Palfrey, Simon and Tiffany Stern. *Shakespeare in Parts*. Oxford: Oxford University Press, 2007.

Peltonen, Markku. *The Duel in Early Modern England: Civility, Politeness and Honour*. Cambridge: Cambridge University Press, 2003.

Rebhorn, Wayne. *Courtly Performances: Masking and Festivity in Castiglione's Book of the Courtier*. Detroit: Wayne State University Press, 1978.

Rebhorn, Wayne. *Foxes and Lions: Machiavelli's Confidence Men*. Ithaca, NY: Cornell University Press, 1988.

Rebhorn, Wayne. *The Emperor of Men's Minds: Literature and the Renaissance Discourse of Rhetoric*. Ithaca, NY: Cornell University Press, 1995.

Rhodes, Neil. *The Power of Eloquence and English Renaissance Literature*. Hemel Hempstead: Harvester Wheatsheaf, 1992.

Richards, Jennifer. 'Assumed Simplicity and the Critique of Nobility: Or, How Castiglione Read Cicero'. *Renaissance Quarterly* 54 (2001): 460–86.

Richards, Jennifer. *Rhetoric and Courtliness in Early Modern Literature*. Cambridge: Cambridge University Press, 2003.

Richards, Jennifer. *Rhetoric*. The New Critical Idiom. London: Routledge, 2008.

Scaglione, Aldo. *Knights at Court: Courtliness, Chivalry, and Courtesy from Ottonian Germany to the Italian Renaissance*. Berkeley: University of California Press, 1991.

Scragg, Leah. *Discovering Shakespeare's Meaning*. Basingstoke: Palgrave Macmillan, 1998.

Skinner, Quentin. *The Foundations of Modern Political Thought*, 2 vols, vol. 1. *The Renaissance*. Cambridge: Cambridge University Press, 1978.

Skinner, Quentin. *Machiavelli: A Very Short Introduction*. Oxford: Oxford University Press, 1981.

Skinner, Quentin. *Forensic Shakespeare*. Oxford: Oxford University Press, 2014.

Smith, Emma, ed. *Shakespeare's Comedies*. Blackwell Guides to Criticism. Oxford: Blackwell, 2004.

Smith, Emma. *The Cambridge Introduction to Shakespeare*. Cambridge: Cambridge University Press, 2007.

Stone, Lawrence. 'The Educational Revolution in England, 1560–1640'. *Past & Present* 28 (1964): 41–80.

Stone, Lawrence. 'Social Mobility in England, 1500–1700'. *Past & Present* 33 (1966): 16–55.

Stone, Lawrence. *The Crisis of the Aristocracy 1558–1641*. Oxford: Oxford University Press, 1967.

Taylor, Charles. *Sources of the Self: The Making of the Modern Identity*. Cambridge: Cambridge University Press, 1989.

Thirsk, Joan. *Economic Policy and Projects: The Development of a Consumer Society in Early Modern England*. Oxford: Clarendon, 1978.

Thomas, Keith. 'Work and Leisure'. *Past & Present* 29 (1964): 51–62.

Thomas, Keith. 'Honour and Reputation'. *The Ends of Life:*

Roads to Fulfilment in Early Modern England. Oxford: Oxford
  University Press, 2009, 147–86.
Vickers, Brian. '"The Power of Persuasion": Images of the Orator,
  Elyot to Shakespeare'. *Renaissance Eloquence: Studies in
  the Theory and Practice of Renaissance Rhetoric,* ed. James
  J. Murphy. Berkeley: University of California Press, 1983,
  411–35.
Vickers, Brian. *In Defence of Rhetoric.* Oxford: Clarendon Press,
  1988.
Watson, Curtis Brown. *Shakespeare and the Renaissance Concept
  of Honor.* Westport, CT: Greenwood Press, 1976.
Whigham, Frank. *Ambition and Privilege: The Social Tropes of
  Elizabethan Courtesy Theory.* Berkeley: University of California
  Press, 1984.
Wiles, David. *Shakespeare's Clown: Actor and Text in the
  Elizabethan Playhouse.* Cambridge: Cambridge University Press,
  1987.
Woodhouse, J. R. *Baldesar Castiglione: A Reassessment of The
  Courtier.* Edinburgh: Edinburgh University Press, 1978.
Wrightson, Keith. *English Society, 1580–1680.* New Brunswick,
  NJ: Rutgers University Press, 1982.
Wrightson, Keith. 'Estates, Degrees, and Sorts: Changing
  Perceptions of Society in Tudor and Stuart England'. *Language,
  History and Class,* ed. Penelope J. Corfield. Oxford: Basil
  Blackwell, 1991, 30–52.

Performance criticism

Cartmell, Deborah. *Interpreting Shakespeare on Screen.*
  Basingstoke: Palgrave Macmillan, 2000.
Jackson, Russell, ed. *The Cambridge Companion to Shakespeare on
  Film.* Cambridge: Cambridge University Press, 2000.
Jorgens, Jack J. *Shakespeare on Film.* Bloomington: Indiana
  University Press, 1979.
Shaughnessy, Robert, ed. *Shakespeare on Film.* New Casebooks.
  Basingstoke: Palgrave Macmillan, 1998.
Wells, Stanley, ed. *The Cambridge Companion to Shakespeare on
  Stage.* Cambridge: Cambridge University Press, 2009.

Worthen, W. B. 'Deeper Meanings and Theatrical Technique: The Rhetoric of Performance Criticism'. *Shakespeare Quarterly* 40 (1989): 441–55.

Editions of the play

Much Ado About Nothing, ed. Sheldon P. Zitner. The Oxford Shakespeare. Oxford: Oxford University Press, 1993.

Much Ado About Nothing, ed. F. H. Mares. The New Cambridge Shakespeare. Cambridge: Cambridge University Press, 2003.

Much Ado About Nothing, ed. R. A. Foakes. The Penguin Shakespeare. London: Penguin, 2005.

Much Ado About Nothing. *The Norton Shakespeare: Comedies*, ed. Stephen Greenblatt, Walter Cohen, Jean E. Howard and Katharine Eisaman Maus, 2nd edn. New York: W. W. Norton, 2008, 566–620.

Much Ado About Nothing, ed. Jonathan Bate and Eric Rasmussen. The RSC Shakespeare. Basingstoke: Palgrave Macmillan, 2009.

Much Ado About Nothing, ed. Claire McEachern, rev. edn. The Arden Shakespeare, 3rd series. London: Bloomsbury Arden Shakespeare, 2016.

Films and theatrical performances

Love's Labour's Won or Much Ado About Nothing. Directed by Christopher Luscombe. A Royal Shakespeare Company Production, 2015.

Much Ado About Nothing. Directed by Kenneth Branagh. Renaissance Films/Samuel Goldwyn Production, 1993.

Much Ado About Nothing. Directed by Joss Whedon. Bellwether Pictures, 2012.

Much Ado About Nothing. Directed by Jeremy Herrin. A Shakespeare's Globe Production, 2012.

Websites

Shakespeare's Words

http://shakespeareswords.com/

This is a site based on the book *Shakespeare's Words: A Glossary and Language Companion* compiled by David Crystal and Ben Crystal (London: Penguin, 2002). The Crystals, father and son, are the leading authorities on early modern English.

Concordance of Shakespeare's complete works

http://www.opensourceshakespeare.org/concordance/

This site enables one to search for specific words in the entire works of Shakespeare.

Early Books Online (EEBO)

http://eebo.chadwyck.com/home

EEBO contains the vast majority of the titles printed in English between 1475 and 1700 in digital facsimile form. It is an indispensable resource for scholars all over the world, allowing them to gain access to early modern sources without having to travel to one of the few libraries that possess the texts. Many university libraries have taken out subscriptions to EEBO.

World Shakespeare Bibliography

www.worldshakesbib.org

World Shakespeare Bibliography is a database with one of the most exhaustive records of Shakespeare scholarship and theatre productions from 1960 onwards.

JSTOR Understanding Shakespeare

http://labs.jstor.org/shakespeare/

This is a useful research tool that lists all articles on JSTOR, the important digital library, in connection with each play by Shakespeare. The articles are linked to the relevant line in the text.

.